BEHOLD THE LAMB

R. Kent Hughes

While this book is designed for the reader's personal enjoyment and profit, it is also intended for group study. A Leader's Guide with Victor Multiuse Transparency Masters is available from your local bookstore or from the publisher.

VICTOR BOOKS®

A DIVISION OF SCRIPTURE PRESS PUBLICATIONS INC.
USA CANADA ENGLAND

Second printing, 1987

Unless otherwise noted, Scripture quotations are from the *New American Standard Bible,* © the Lockman Foundation 1960, 1962, 1963, 1968, 1971, 1972, 1973, 1975, 1977. Other quotations are from the *Holy Bible: New International Version* (NIV), © 1973, 1978, 1984, International Bible Society. Used by permission of Zondervan Bible Publishers; *The Living Bible* (TLB), © 1971, Tyndale House Publishers, Wheaton, IL 60189. Used by permission. The *King James Version* (KJV); *The New Testament in Modern English, Revised Edition,* (PH), © J. B. Phillips, 1958, 1960, 1972, permission of Macmillan Publishing Co. and Collins Publishers; *The New English Bible* (NEB), © 1961 and 1970, Oxford University Press and Cambridge University Press; *The Modern Language Bible: The Berkeley Version in Modern English* (MLB), © 1945, 1959, 1969 by Zondervan Publishing House. Used by permission.

Recommended Dewey Decimal Classification: 226.5
  Suggested Subject Heading: JOHN

Library of Congress Catalog Card Number: 83-51299
ISBN: 0-88207-623-X

VICTOR BOOKS
A division of SP Publications, Inc.
          Wheaton, Illinois 60187

Contents

FOREWORD

To bring fresh treasures from the Gospel of John is no small accomplishment. Yet this is what Kent Hughes has done in this book.

Bible study groups, Sunday School classes, and individual Christians will benefit from the author's careful study and interest-heightening writing.

"What does it mean to be a Christian, a child of God?" This is the question Dr. Hughes seems to be answering throughout these studies. His warm exposition of John's Gospel makes this book especially helpful for those who have not yet entered the kingdom, as well as those who have entered and are still excited to learn what it all means.

One unusual feature of this book—elevating it above many others—is the number of windows on the truth the author provides out of his extensive reading and rich personal and pastoral experience. These range from Warren Wiersbe to Phil Donahue, Ingmar Bergman to Kenneth Chafin, as well as A. W. Tozer, Donald Grey Barnhouse, F. B. Meyer, G. Campbell Morgan and, of course, C. S. Lewis.

As I have read this book, I've been impressed with a sense of immediacy, even of urgency, as if the author were trying to make me feel the experience of Jesus' life and teaching in the Fourth Gospel. Not just understand, but feel.

I wish you could know Kent Hughes, rather than merely read his words. He is my pastor and friend: I know that his words proceed from a life that seeks to "adorn the doctrine of God our Saviour in all things."

Joseph Bayly
Bartlett, Illinois

To Brea-Olinda Friends
who first shared my joy
in opening the great themes of John

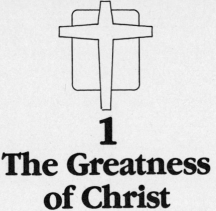

1
The Greatness
of Christ

The Gospel of John is unique in its powerful presentation of Jesus as the great Creator-God of the universe, and has been used countless times to open the eyes of unbelievers to see Him as Saviour. The book's continuing effect on Christians is equally profound as believers find it an ongoing source for expanding their concepts of the Saviour's greatness. Each time the serious student returns to the Gospel of John, his view of Christ will be a little bigger—something like Lucy's experience with the lion Aslan (the Christ symbol in C.S. Lewis' *Chronicles of Narnia*):

> As she again gazed into his large wise face, he said, "Welcome, child."
> "Aslan," said Lucy, "you're bigger."
> "That is because you are older, little one," answered he.
> "Not because you are?"
> "I am not. But every year you grow, you will find me bigger"
> (*Prince Caspian*, Collins, p. 124).

My hope is that as we work our way through the wonders of the Gospel of John our view of Christ will be bigger and bigger and bigger.

The *prolog* (vv. 1-18) is considered one of the most sublime sections in Scripture. Some believe that it was the "Hymn of the Incarnate Word," sung in the early church, for Christ's incarnation is its subject and it is marvelously poetic. Yet it is more. It introduces the major ideas of the book: the cosmic Christ coming as light into the world, suffering rejection, but pouring "grace upon grace" to those who receive Him. It emphasizes the matchless greatness of Christ (vv. 1-3), the greatness of Christ's love (vv. 4-13), and the greatness of His grace (vv. 14-18). The opening words almost bend under the weight they are made to bear. The force of their meaning is staggering:

> In the beginning was the Word, and the Word was with God, and the Word was God. He was in the beginning with God. All things came into being through Him; and apart from Him nothing came into being that has come into being (vv. 1-3).

Eternally Preexistent

"In the beginning was the Word" clearly tells us that there never was a time when Christ did not exist. The verb *was* is in the Greek imperfect tense which means "was continuing." In fact the entire verse bears this sense: "In the beginning was continuing the Word, and the Word was continuing with God, and the Word was continually God."

This kind of thinking makes for a super headache. Our minds look backward until time disappears and thought collapses in exhaustion: God and Jesus Christ are eternal in *relationship*. "And the Word was with God" literally means "the Word was continually toward God." The Father and the Son were continually face to face. The word *with* bears the idea of nearness, along with the sense of movement toward God, which is to say that there existed the deepest equality and intimacy in the Holy Trinity.

Eternally God

The final phrase, "And the Word was God" tells us that the Word (Jesus) was God in essence and character. He was God in every way, though He was a separate person from God the Father. The phrase perfectly preserves Jesus' identity while stating that He is God. He constantly was God from all eternity.

Some cultists wrongly translate this phrase to say, "And the Word was *a* god" (Jehovah's Witnesses, *The New World Translation of the Holy Scriptures*). They do this by supplying the indefinite article *a* where there is none in the Greek. While this is proper to do in some situations, it is wrong here because John is stressing the essence of the Word.

In Greek grammar, when there is no definite article before a noun, the noun describes the character and quality of the person. If John had said the Word was *the* God, that would have meant that the Word was perfectly identical with God, thus contradicting the scriptural doctrine of the Trinity. In stating the Word *was* God, without the definite article, he is saying that the Word was of the very same essence and being as God. This grammatical construction perfectly states that Jesus is 100 percent God, while affirming His position as the separate, second person of the Holy Trinity.

This simple sentence dealing with the eternalness of Christ is the most compact theological statement in all of Scripture. From it we understand that Jesus existed as God from all eternity, in perfect fellowship with God the Father and, (though not mentioned) the Holy Spirit. Even that is not all. Verse 3 leaves no doubt that Jesus is the Creator of the universe: "All things came into being through Him; and apart from Him nothing came into being that has come into being." That Christ is Creator is the consistent witness of the New Testament:

For by Him all things were created, both in the heavens and on earth, visible and invisible, whether thrones or dominions or rulers or authorities—all things have been created through Him and for Him. And He is before all things, and in Him all things hold together (Col. 1:16-17).

God . . . in these last days has spoken to us in His Son, whom He appointed heir of all things, through whom also He made the world. And He is the radiance of His glory and the exact representation of His nature, and upholds all things by the word of His power (Heb. 1:1-3).

Worthy art Thou, our Lord and our God, to receive glory and honor and power; for Thou didst create all things, and because of Thy will they existed, and were created (Rev. 4:11).

Yet for us there is but one God, the Father, from whom are all things, and we exist for Him; and one Lord, Jesus Christ, through whom are all things, and we exist through Him (1 Cor. 8:6).

Keeping in mind that Christ is Creator, think of this: The average galaxy contains about 100 billion stars and there are at least 100 million galaxies in known space. Einstein believed that we have scanned with our largest telescopes only one-billionth of theoretical space. This means that there are probably something like 10 octillion stars in space. How many is that? One thousand thousands is one million; 1,000 millions is one billion; 1,000 billions is one trillion; 1,000 trillions is one quadrillion; 1,000 quadrillions is one quintillion; 1,000 quintillions is one sextillion; 1,000 sextillions is one septillion; 1,000 septillions is one octillion. Jesus created them all.

He is the Creator not only of the visible universe but also of the microcosms within the universe. The verse from Colossians tells us He holds all of this together. Because He is Creator, He knows what His creatures need. We can entrust our lives to Him. Considering the greatness of Christ, nothing else makes sense.

The Greatness of Christ's Love

The greatness of Christ's love is apparent from the opening line of John where He is mystically identified as "the Word." Though much can be said about this term because of its rich history in Greek literature, its main significance here is that *Christ has always sought to reveal Himself.* An interpretative paraphrase could well read, "In the beginning was the Communication." That Christ was always the Word should remind us that He has always been love, for the very nature of love is to express itself—to find an object.

The metaphor of Christ as light stresses the revelation, rejection, and reception of His love as it came to the world. Notice the occurrences of the word *light:*

> In Him was life; and the life was the light of men. And the light shines in the darkness; and the darkness did not comprehend it. There came a man, sent from God, whose name was John. He came for a witness, that he might bear witness of the light, that all might believe through him. He was not the light, but came that he might bear witness of the light. There was the true light which, coming into the world, enlightens every man. He was in the world, and the world was made through Him, and the world did not know Him. He came to His own, and those who were His own did not receive Him. But as many as received Him, to them He gave the right to become children of God, even to those who believe in His name: who were born not of blood, nor of the will of the flesh, nor of the will of man, but of God (John 1:4-13).

Light Revealed

In clearest terms, Christ is described as light. "In Him was life; and the life was the light of men. And the light shines in the darkness" (vv. 4-5).

We know from Scripture that Christ is light in a physical sense, for He appears as such in glory (Matt. 17:2; Mark 9:2; John 17:5); but emphasis here is on His being spiritual light to

Light exposes darkness

a dark (sinful) world. All humanity benefits from the light. "There was the true light which, coming into the world, enlightens every man" (v. 9). This happens through nature and conscience (Rom. 1:19-20).

The thought of our Lord being spiritual light gives us a heartening insight into His loving attempt to reach the world. Where light goes darkness is dispelled, revealing the true nature of life. No place with the slightest crack is safe from its presence. Our text says that "the light shines in the darkness," which literally means it shines continually in the darkness. Christ, then, bombards every little chink in our hearts of darkness through the work of His Holy Spirit in nature, conscience, and the Scriptures. Meditating on Christ being light helps believer and unbeliever better understand how much He loves us.

Light Rejected

The majority of mankind rejected the light. "And the darkness did not comprehend it" (v. 5), or more accurately as the margin reads, "did not overpower it." The light met with tremendous resistance:

> He was in the world, and the world was made through Him, and the world did not know Him. He came to His own, and those who were His own did not receive Him (vv. 10-11).

The One who said, "Let there be light," the One whose love constrained Him to shine His saving light through creation and conscience, the One who mercifully sheathed His light in a human body that He might bring light to men, the One who set aside a special people for Himself to be a light to the nations, the "Sunrise from on high," was rejected! Yet today, He still persists as light, seeking His way into hostile hearts. And some respond.

Light Received

> But as many as received Him, to them He gave the right to become children of God, even to those who believe in His name: who were born not of blood, nor of the will of the flesh, nor of the will of man, but of God (vv. 12-13).

Those who receive the light become children of God. This is a stupendous truth. Apparently John never got over it, because when he was an old man he wrote, "See how great a love the Father has bestowed on us, that we should be called the children of God; and such we are" (1 John 3:1). "And such we are" ought to be the refrain of our lives—if we have believed in Him.

What is more, the future holds out to us as children the bright prospect of becoming like the risen Christ. John followed his statement with another of even greater wonder:

> Beloved, now we are children of God, and it has not appeared as yet what we shall be. We know that, when He appears, we shall be like Him, because we shall see Him just as He is (1 John 3:2).

C.S. Lewis, in his great sermon "The Weight of Glory" which he preached at St. Mary's, Oxford, expanded the implications of being children of God:

> It is a serious thing to live in a society of possible gods and goddesses, to remember that the dullest and most uninteresting person you talk to may one day be a creature which, if you saw it now, you would be strongly tempted to worship, or else a horror and a corruption such as you now meet, if at all, only in a nightmare. All day long we are, in some degree, helping each other to one or other of these destinations. It is in the light of these overwhelming possibilities, it is with the awe and the circumspection proper to them, that we should conduct all our dealings with one another, all friendships, all loves, all play, all

politics. There are no *ordinary* people (*The Weight of Glory and Other Addresses,* Eerdmans, p. 15).

As we relate this to the world, it must be done with simplicity. We become one of God's own by "believing in His name," which means believing that Jesus is the eternal Creator who became one of us, took our sins on Himself, died on the cross, rose from the dead, and is again with God the Father.

The Greatness of Christ's Grace

At the close of John's prolog, the word *grace* is prominent:

> And the Word became flesh, and dwelt among us, and we beheld His glory, glory as of the only begotten from the Father, full of grace and truth. . . . For of His fullness we have all received, and grace upon grace. For the Law was given through Moses; grace and truth were realized through Jesus Christ (vv. 14, 16-17).

When Jesus became flesh and dwelt (literally, "pitched His tent") in the midst of humanity, His glory was characterized as "full of grace and truth."

"Grace upon grace" (v. 16) literally is "grace instead of grace." How do we get grace instead of grace? As the grace we receive is appropriated, more will come, and then more, and even more. Other helpful translations read, "grace following grace," "grace heaped on grace" as they convey the idea that grace continues to overflow. Martin Luther expressed it this way:

> The sun is not dimmed and darkened by shining on so many people or by providing the entire world with its light and splendor. It retains its light intact. It loses nothing; it is immeasurable, perhaps able to illumine ten more worlds. I suppose that a hundred thousand candles can be ignited from one light, and still this light will not lose any of its brilliance. . . . Thus Christ, our Lord, to whom we must flee and of whom we must ask all, is an intermina-

ble well, the chief source of all grace. . . . Even if the whole world were to draw from this fountain enough grace and truth to transform all people into angels, still it would not lose as much as a drop. This fountain constantly overflows with sheer grace (Ewald M. Plass, *What Luther Says,* Vol. 2, Concordia, pp. 614-615)

This grace is readily available to all as Paul wrote, "Where sin increased, grace abounded all the more" (Rom. 5:20).

The prolog concludes: "No man has seen God at any time; the only begotten God, who is in the bosom of the Father, He has explained Him" (v. 18). Jesus is the explanation (the exegesis) of God the Father. The greatness of Christ explains the greatness of the Father; the greatness of Christ's love explains the greatness of the Father's love; and the greatness of Christ's grace explains the greatness of the Father's grace.

If we would see the Father, we must focus on the Son— "Behold the Lamb."

2
Essentials of Witness

When John the Baptist began his public ministry, as the supreme witness of all time, he was eminently prepared. His life was focused on Christ from before his birth, and he had spent much time alone with God.

The Angel Gabriel had appeared to Zacharias, the aged priest, and told him that the son to be born to him and Elizabeth would be filled with the Spirit, not only after his birth, but while he was still in his mother's womb:

> He will turn back many of the sons of Israel to the Lord their God. And it is he who will go as a forerunner before Him in the spirit and power of Elijah (Luke 1:16-17).

At the day of John's naming, Zacharias sang the "Benedictus" which ends in these words:

> And you, child, will be called the prophet of the Most High; for you will go on before the Lord to prepare His ways; to give to His people the knowledge of salvation by the forgiveness of their sins (Luke 1:76-77).

John's life from that time until he began his public ministry is summed up for us in one verse: "And the child grew and was spiritually strengthened, and was in the deserts until the time of his appearing to Israel" (Luke 1:80, MLB).

The focus on the Messiah during John's early years is apparent in his way of life and in his message. His message contained essential elements of witness that can help us more clearly focus on Christ and be more effective witnesses.

Essentials in the Messenger

John had been preaching for over a year and his ministry had changed the Palestinian world. Multitudes had come to hear him and to be baptized. Matthew tells us that even King Herod sought him and almost believed.

Toward the end of John's year of preaching, Jesus visited him and asked to be baptized. At first John refused, but then deferred to Jesus' request. As he baptized Jesus, John saw the Holy Spirit come upon our Lord and heard God's words, "Thou art My beloved Son, in Thee I am well-pleased" (Luke 3:22).

During the forty days following the baptism of Jesus, John's world became a ferment as he preached about the Messiah with increasing fervor. When they could stand it no longer, the religious leaders in Jerusalem sent a delegation, something like a congressional fact-finding committee, to find out who John was and what he was saying:

> And this is the witness of John, when the Jews sent to him priests and Levites from Jerusalem to ask him, "Who are you?" And he confessed and did not deny, and he confessed, "I am not the Christ" (John 1:19-20).

John knew exactly what information they were after—they weren't the first to wonder whether he was the Christ. Carefully he answered that he was not the Messiah. If indeed, John had claimed to be the Christ, the Maccabeans would have unfurled their banners and the world would have been at war.

The delegation's next question was, "What then? Are you Elijah?" (v. 21) That was a fair query since he looked like Elijah and came in the spirit and power of Elijah, whose return the Jews expected before the terrible Day of the Lord (Mal. 4:5-6).

When John answered that he was not Elijah, they asked, "Are you the Prophet?" (John 1:21) referring to the One of whom Moses prophesied: "The Lord your God will raise up for you a Prophet like me from among you, from your countrymen. You shall listen to Him" (Deut. 18:15).

When John replied that he was not the Prophet, they asked, "Who are you, so that we may give an answer to those who sent us? What do you say about yourself?" (John 1:22)

In John the Baptist's answer we find the first essential of a witness. "I am a voice" (v. 23). With these words, John was reaching back 700 years to Isaiah's prophecy:

> The voice of him that crieth in the wilderness, "Prepare ye the way of the Lord, make straight in the desert a highway for our God" (Isa. 40:3, KJV).

He was saying, "I am not the Word, but a voice. I am not the message, but the communicator. I am not the road, but a workman on the road, making ready the way for Him."

John moved the emphasis away from himself to Jesus: "It is He who comes after me, the thong of whose sandal I am not worthy to untie" (John 1:27).

In these words, John claimed for Jesus a place so exalted that ordinary people like himself were unworthy to perform a task relegated to the lowest slaves. Yet John was among the greatest of men. Jesus said of him: "Truly, I say to you, among those born of women there has not arisen anyone greater than John the Baptist" (Matt. 11:11).

John was a Nazarite from his birth. He never cut his hair. He never touched a dead body. He never drank the fruit of the vine. He had been filled with the Holy Spirit before his birth and nothing was ever to contaminate him.

If ever a man might have felt he had reason to vaunt himself, it was John. He could have talked about his near-miraculous birth, or about the rigors of his solitary life of self-denial in the wilderness. He could have held forth on survival tactics or discussed his unusual diet. He could have recommended his devotional regimen or suggested that he publish a manual of discipline for those who wanted to follow God.

John must have faced this temptation, and to his everlasting credit, he didn't give into it. A witness never obscures or detracts from the one about whom he witnesses.

A friend from my seminary days was asked to deliver the sermon at the Hollywood Bowl sunrise service. As he sat with the planning committee, they asked him, "Where can the helicopter pick you up?"

He replied that he didn't think there was room in his neighborhood for a helicopter to land. They told him that the man who had spoken the year before had to have a helicopter.

When they offered him a police escort, he had visions of flashing lights and motorcycles in front of his house at three in the morning, ready to escort him in his Volvo to the Hollywood Bowl. Again he turned them down.

Such self-aggrandizement is far removed from the pattern set by John the Baptist who said, "He must increase, but I must decrease" (John 3:30). The servant of Christ does not exalt himself, knowing that he is but a third-level rower in the galley.

Exemplifying the same attitude, the Apostle Paul wrote, "Let a man regard us in this manner, as servants of Christ" (1 Cor. 4:1).

Arturo Toscanini had conducted his orchestra in a brilliant performance of Beethoven's Ninth Symphony. The audience clapped, whistled, and stamped their feet. As the ovation began to subside, Toscanini turned toward the musicians and looked at them intently. He seemed almost out of control as he whispered: "Gentlemen! Gentlemen!" The orchestra members leaned forward to listen. Was he angry? They could not tell. In a fiercely enunciated whisper, Toscanini said, "Gentlemen, I am nothing." That was an extraordinary admission, since Toscanini was blessed with enormous gifts. He went on, "Gentlemen, you are nothing." They had heard that before during rehearsals. Then, in a tone of adoration, Toscanini said, "But Beethoven, he is everything, everything, *everything!*" (Vernon C. Grounds, "Faith to Faith Failure, or What's So Good about Success?" *Christianity Today*, Dec. 9, 1977)

We need this kind of perspective about ourselves and the Lord Jesus Christ. We are nothing. He is everything. That was John's attitude. It is the attitude of an authentic messenger of Christ.

Essentials in the Message
The next day he saw Jesus coming to him, and said, "Behold the Lamb of God who takes away the sin of the world!" (John 1:29)

In this one sentence is the essence of the Christian message. It is difficult for Westerners to appreciate the power of John's words. For the Jewish people of that day, these words carried overpowering significance.

When John's audience heard his words about the Lamb of God, they most likely thought back to Abraham and Isaac, when young Isaac had asked his father, "Behold the fire and the wood, but where is the lamb?" Abraham had replied, "God will provide Himself the lamb for the burnt offering, my son" (Gen. 22:7-8). They would have remembered the Passover lamb, its blood applied to the doorposts, or the beautiful phrases from Isaiah:

All of us like sheep have gone astray, each of us has turned to his own way; but the Lord has caused the iniquity of us all to fall on Him. He was oppressed and He was afflicted, yet He did not open His mouth; like a lamb that is led to slaughter, and like a sheep that is silent before its shearers, so He did not open His mouth (53:6-7).

John was telling them that Jesus was to be the sacrifice for their sins, God's provision for their deepest need.

Our message must be the same as John's. It may seem unnecessary to say that we must focus on the Lamb of God, but history proves that we need to be reminded. It is dangerously easy to move away from the blood of the Atonement. Many of us still love William Cowper's great hymn, "There Is a Fountain Filled with Blood," yet I have heard Cowper excoriated and his hymn almost spat on by people who considered themselves Christians. How easy to abandon this essential truth:

> There is a fountain filled with blood
> Drawn from Immanuel's veins,
> And sinners plunged beneath that flood
> Lose all their guilty stains.

The reality of the Atonement must be primary in our witness. Christ came to give abundant life, but that in itself is not the Gospel. He worked miracles and is still able to do so today, but that alone is not the Gospel. These truths are benefits of the Good News which centers on Christ as the *Sinbearer,* the Lamb of God who takes away the sin of the world.

While it is important to understand the doctrine of the Atonement, it is absolutely essential for salvation to *experience* it—for each of us to acknowledge that Christ died for us.

Christ the Lamb has been the eternal message. Abraham prophesied His sacrifice. The Passover applied the principle of His sacrifice. Isaiah personified His sacrifice. John the Baptist identified the sacrifice. And the Revelation of John the Apostle magnified His sacrifice.

In a San Diego art museum I stood before a painting of a lamb with a faint halo around its head. The lamb's legs were tied and it was lying on a cross. It was titled *Agnus Dei,* "The Lamb of God," and its date was 1525. I stood before the picture for a long time, filled with deep emotion. It was not just the beauty that held me, but the fact of the Atonement, and the words of John the Baptist, "Behold, the Lamb of God who takes away the sin of the world!" (John 1:29)

Effect of Witness

A faithful witness tells how to appropriate the benefits of the Lamb. John the Baptist said, "In order that He might be manifested to Israel, I came baptizing in water" (John 1:31).

John's water baptism signified repentance. People were to turn from their sins so that they would be ready to receive the Messiah and His benefits. Christ brought a new baptism:

> And John bore witness saying, "I have beheld the Spirit descending as a dove out of heaven; and He remained upon Him. And I did not recognize Him, but He who sent me to baptize in water said to me, 'He upon whom you see the Spirit descending and remaining upon Him, this is the One who baptizes in the Holy Spirit' " (vv. 32-33).

John's baptism motivated people to change. Christ's baptism brought the power to change. That marvelous word *baptism,* which essentially means a dipping or submersion, extends to the spiritual. The Apostle Paul spoke of that spiritual immersion: "For by one Spirit we were all baptized into one body" (1 Cor. 12:13).

This saturation of the Holy Spirit comes at the time of salvation. Power to change our lives, to leave our sin, to enjoy fullness of life comes from a soaking or immersion in the Holy Spirit.

Many people miss knowing Christ because they have never truly repented. It is possible to give lip service to the idea of His sacrificial atonement without fully acknowledging the need of it personally. Yet grace without repentance is cheap grace. If we truly believe, we have both the realization of what Christ has done and a repentence from sin.

3
The Lord Is in This Place

Because we can't flick a switch and produce spiritual realities in living color, we too often ignore them. Life has become so desupernaturalized that we do not see God. We go to work and do not know His presence. We go to school and do not see Him. At home, in our friendships, wherever we are, God is there but we do not know it.

This mentality intrudes right into the church, so that we can sing great hymns, pray together, and not really know that He is there. Because of our blindness, our Christianity becomes an empty, dull religion that is interesting to no one. What can we do about this? A look at the first encounter between Jesus and Nathanael may offer some answers.

The Lord Was With Nathanael

After Jesus' baptism and temptation, He began to call His disciples. After He had chosen Andrew, Peter, and Philip from Bethsaida, Philip went to his friend Nathanael:

> "We have found Him, of whom Moses in the Law and also the Prophets wrote, Jesus of Nazareth, the son of Joseph." And

> Nathanael said to him, "Can any good thing come out of Naza-
> reth?" Philip said to him, "Come and see" (John 1:45-46).

Philip was so excited that the words must have tumbled out of his mouth. Nathanael had not heard about Jesus, but he knew the Old Testament. He knew that Bethlehem was to be the birthplace of the Messiah, not Nazareth. Besides, Nazareth was just four miles from Cana, Nathanael's hometown, and since there was rivalry between the towns, he questioned, "Can any good thing come out of Nazareth?" (1:46)

Philip gave the best and only possible response: "Come and see"—one to remember when we are tempted to argue.

Jesus saw them coming, and called out, "Behold, an Israelite indeed, in whom is no guile!" (1:47)

Nathanael asked, "How do You know me?" (v. 48) "How do You know what I am like—that I am guileless?"

Jesus didn't spend time on the preliminaries with Nathanael but rather got right to the essentials. Jesus wanted Nathanael to know that He saw how transparent and honest he was. And Nathanael, being a man without guile, owned up to it.

Notice that Jesus said Nathanael was an Israelite in whom there was no guile. Jesus' words were meant to make Nathanael think back to Jacob for, like all Jews, Nathanael knew that the patriarch Jacob had been full of guile. Jacob had used his guile to cheat his brother, Esau, out of his birthright and had run away because he feared his brother would kill him. That night, alone and terrified in the wilderness, Jacob had put a stone under his head and gone to sleep. God came to him in a vision:

> And he had a dream, and behold, a ladder was set on the earth
> with its top reaching to heaven; and behold, the angels of God
> were ascending and descending on it (Gen. 28:12).

The Lord gave Jacob a promise of posterity and blessing that reaches to this day. When Jacob wakened, he said:

"Surely the Lord is in this place, and I did not know it." And he
was afraid and said, "How awesome is this place! This is none
other than the house of God, and this is the gate of heaven"
(Gen. 28:16-17).

God kept working in Jacob's life until finally, after wrestling
with God, he was renamed Israel. In saying that Nathanael had
no guile, Jesus was cleverly acclaiming him as an ideal Israelite.
William Temple's translation of the verse is, "Behold, an Israelite in whom there is no Jacob."

Nathanael must have been reeling—Jesus could read his mind!
But how? And then, as if once were not enough, Jesus said,
"Before Philip called you, when you were under the fig tree, I
saw you" (John 1:48). Nathanael had a religious experience
that only Jesus knew of. It was as if Jesus had said, "I know
about the things you shared only with God." Jesus knew!

Nathanael was not only guileless; he was also intelligent. He
realized from Jesus' statement that Jesus was omniscient; therefore, Jesus had to be God! Nathanael answered Jesus, "Rabbi,
You are the Son of God; You are the King of Israel" (v. 49).
Because he was an Israelite without guile, he was prepared for
the Messiah. When he saw Jesus' omniscience, he responded in
belief.

Jesus said, in effect, "You believed because you saw I am
omniscient? You haven't seen anything yet!"

"Because I said to you that I saw you under the fig tree, do you
believe? You shall see greater things than these. . . . Truly, truly,
I say to you, you shall see the heavens opened, and the angels
of God ascending and descending on the Son of man" (vv. 50-51).

This amazing promise took Nathanael back almost 2,000
years to the story of Jacob and his ladder of angels. But in Jesus'
words to Nathanael, there was no ladder. Rather, the angels
would be ascending and descending on the Son of man.

"Nathanael, as you enter into the fullness of your relationship with Christ, and as your spiritual vision is sharpened, you are going to see the angels and hear the rustle of their wings as they ascend and descend the ladder [Christ] between heaven and earth for you."

The Lord Is With Us!

What an electrifying reality for us! I believe God gives us imagery because images are easy to hold on to, and through the image we touch the reality. As we see Christ as our "ladder" between heaven and earth, we too will hear the rustle of angels' wings.

God came to Jacob when he was exhausted, pillowed on a stone. God is often the closest when He seems farthest away. Out in the wilds of life, in the hard places, God is active in our behalf. The angels do minister to us. In Hebrews we read, "Are they not all ministering spirits, sent out to render service for the sake of those who will inherit salvation?" (1:14)

These ministering spirits are curious at times: "It was revealed to them that they were not serving themselves but you in these things ... things into which angels long to look" (1 Peter 1:12).

I love the medieval paintings in which the sky is full of angels and fat cherubs. The artists captured the reality that Peter was conveying, of angels that want to see what is going on in our world. If our eyes could be opened, we would at times see the sky full of angels.

The Lord Was in New Hebrides

On a dark night in the New Hebrides, a Scottish missionary couple suddenly realized that their house was surrounded by cannibals. The couple spent that terror-filled night praying that God would protect them. As they prayed, they heard the cries of the savages and imagined them coming through the door to kill them. When the sun began to rise, the couple saw that the natives were retreating into the forest. The missionaries were amazed, and they praised God. They continued bravely in their work, and a year later, the chief of that tribe was converted. The missionary asked the chief why he and his men had not killed them on that night. The chief replied in surprise, "Who were all those men with you?"

The missionary answered, "Why, there were no men with us."

The chief began to argue with him, saying, "There were hundreds of tall men in shining garments with drawn swords circling your house, so that we could not attack you" (Billy Graham, *Angels*, Doubleday, p. 3).

The experience of John Paton and his wife was, in a way, a repeat of what happened to the Prophet Elisha. He and his servant were surrounded by the enemy and his servant was terrified. When Elisha prayed that the servant's eyes would be opened, the man saw flaming chariots of fire and the armies of God around them. He saw the reality of the ministering spirits (2 Kings 6:15-17).

That same reality is ours. Someday we will see heaven open and the angels ascending and descending upon the Son of man. In Christ we are brought very near to heaven. In Christ, we live in the suburbs of heaven. The church on earth is an adjunct to heaven and we are fellow-citizens with all the saints:

But you have come to Mount Zion and to the city of the living God, the heavenly Jerusalem, and to myriads of angels, to the general assembly and church of the first-born who are enrolled in heaven, and to God the Judge of all, and to the spirits of righteous men made perfect (Heb. 12:22-23).

Blessed be the God and Father of our Lord Jesus Christ, who has blessed us with every spiritual blessing in the heavenly places in Christ (Eph. 1:3).

For our citizenship is in heaven, from which also we eagerly wait for a Saviour, the Lord Jesus Christ (Phil. 3:20).

All the spiritual blessings are ours—the ministry of angels, our heavenly citizenship, the closeness of heaven. In Jesus' words, "You shall see greater things than these," there is a promise of growth, as we experience the ongoing and growing understanding of heavenly realities around us.

God is infinite and His infinite love will unfold for eternity. We will always be surprised as we grow to new knowledge in His love. His power, His mercy, His strength, His transcendence will be unfolding for us for eternity.

When Nathanael's forebear, Jacob, saw the spiritual realities, he expressed his praise and awe:

"Surely the Lord is in this place, and I did not know it. . . . How awesome is this place! This is none other than the house of God, and this is the gate of heaven" (Gen. 28:16-17).

Jacob realized the spiritual realities. He called that place Bethel, the house of God (vv. 19-22). What a wondrous thing it is to know that "Bethel" is wherever we are. There is commerce between heaven and earth on our behalf—the rustle of angels' wings in our lives. What a difference it will make if we appropriate these spiritual realities in all our living. The great problem is simply believing what we believe. We believe it, but do we *believe* it? I pray that God will help us to see His angelic care.

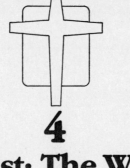

4
Christ: The Wine of Life

The Hebrew wedding celebration was the grand event in life, especially among the poor. The marriage ceremony took place late in the evening, following a feast. After the ceremony, the bride and groom were escorted to their home in a torchlight parade complete with a canopy over their heads. They took the longest route possible, so that everyone would have opportunity to wish them well. Instead of a honeymoon, they held open house for a week. They were addressed as king and queen, wore crowns, and were dressed in their nuptial robes. Their word was considered to be law. For people whose lives would contain much poverty and difficulty, this was a supreme occasion. Many would plod through life and never again have a celebration equal to their wedding.

When the Wine Runs Out
Wine was essential at the Jewish wedding feast because it was a symbol of exhilaration and celebration. It was of such importance that guests could institute a lawsuit if no wine was provided. Those behind the scene at the wedding of Cana were shattered by this breakdown in hospitality. Their dreams of hosting the perfect wedding were about to dissolve.

With this background, we can hear distress in Mary's words, "They have no wine" (John 2:3). The drama of the moment was real and intense, and provides the setting for our Lord's first miracle—the beginning of Jesus' signs. When John used the word *sign,* he always spoke of a miracle with a deeper teaching. Here we see not only Christ's power to change physical elements but also His power to change lives. The miracle at Cana is a joyous story of what Christ can do for a person who wants fullness of life.

"They have no wine" goes beyond the lack of refreshment at the Cana wedding. It defines human experience without Christ. Life without Christ is life without wine. In Scripture, wine is a symbol of joy, as in Psalm 104:15: "Wine, which makes man's heart glad," and in the invitation of Isaiah:

> "Ho! Everyone who thirsts, come to the waters; And you who have no money, come, buy and eat. Come, buy wine and milk without money and without cost" (55:1).

Or the beautiful verse in which the vine asks, "Shall I leave my new wine, which cheers God and men, and go wave over the trees?" (Judges 9:13)

To the Jewish people, wine symbolized joy. The rabbis had a saying: "Without wine, there is no joy." At the wedding in Cana, the joy had run out.

The universal experience of mankind, apart from Christ, is that a time comes when the wine runs out, when the joy and exhilaration of life are gone. An example of this in our own time is the life of Ernest Hemingway.

Hemingway had a brilliant mind. His great stories like *The Old Man and the Sea* show his genius. From his early years, he went after everything that life could give him. He was a newspaper reporter and an ambulance driver during World War I. He was involved in the Spanish Civil War and his friendships ranged from bullfighters to authors. Whatever he did, he went for all of it. He went after the natural wines of life, but there came the day when those wines ran out. In Carlos Baker's biography of Hemingway, we read these final words:

> Sunday morning dawned bright and cloudless. Ernest awoke early as always. He put on the red "Emperor's robe" and padded softly down the carpeted stairway. The early sunlight lay in pools on the living room floor. He had noticed that the guns were locked up in the basement. But the keys, as he well knew, were on the window ledge above the kitchen sink. He tiptoed down the basement stairs and unlocked the storage room. It smelled as dank as a grave. He chose a double-barreled shotgun with a tight choke. He had used it for years of pigeon shooting. He took some shells from one of the boxes in the storage room, closed and locked the door and climbed the basement stairs. If he saw the bright day outside, it did not deter him. He crossed the living room to the front foyer, a shrinelike entryway five feet by seven, with oak-paneled walls and a floor of linoleum tile. . . . He slipped in two shells, lowered the gun butt carefully to the floor, leaned forward, pressed the twin barrels against his forehead just above the eyebrows and tripped both triggers (*Ernest Hemingway, A Life Story*, Scribners, pp. 563-64).

Sooner or Later

No matter who we are or what we have tasted of life, a time comes when the exhilarations and excitements of life wear out. For some it comes sooner; for others, later. Often it is when life is at its very best—when a person has health, wealth, friends, and pleasures—that the wine fails and life loses its sparkle. It can happen during the teen years. It is epidemic during the college years. It is endemic to the middle years, and ultimately catches up with everyone. For the person who focuses on life's exhilarations, failure is inevitable. People cope with disappointment in different ways, and most are not as extreme as Hemingway. Many settle for gray days; they clench their fists, and determine to go on with life. Some fight. Others turn bitter and sour.

We need to understand that there is nothing intrinsically wrong with the natural joys of life. The visual wines of life are fine, but there comes a time when we have seen everything we want to, and there is nothing left to bring us excitement.

The wines of the intellect are in some ways more enduring, but they have a built-in defect. The writer of the Book of Ecclesiastes observed:

> I said to myself, "Behold, I have magnified and increased wisdom more than all who were over Jerusalem before me; and my mind has observed a wealth of wisdom and knowledge." And I set my mind to know wisdom and to know madness and folly; I realized that this also is striving after wind. Because in much wisdom there is much grief, and increasing knowledge results in increasing pain (1:16-18).

Intellectual pursuits are a double-edged sword. They can bring great joys, but they can bring early disillusionment.

The sensate wines also run out. It is an axiom of life that the greater the sensual focus, the greater the tendency to boredom.

Christ Serves the Wine of Joy

What was the solution when the wine ran out in Cana? Jesus' mother went to her Son to tell Him of the problem. And then she reported back to the hosts of the wedding, "Whatever He says to you, do it" (John 2:5).

What Jesus did was to produce 180 gallons of wine! What a wedding gift!

He told the servants to fill with water six waterpots which were used for purification rites. Each waterpot held thirty gallons. We know from the Dead Sea Scrolls that those stone pots were used for the ritual of washing the guests.

In His use of these waterpots for the miracle, Jesus was saying that the old ritual was dead and that He was filling the urns with new life. F. F. Bruce wrote that Christ was "changing the water of Jewish purification into the wine of the new age" (*Second Thoughts on the Dead Sea Scrolls,* Eerdmans, p. 135).

Jesus is the giver of abundant joy. For His first miracle, He chose to deal in gladness. He takes the natural joys of life, lifts them up, and ennobles them. He makes them even more enjoyable.

Life has its sorrows. Christ Himself was a Man acquainted with grief. He knew all about sorrow, but the overall tenor of His life was joy, and this is what He wants for His followers. Shortly before His death He said, "These things I have spoken to you, that My joy may be in you, and that your joy may be made full" (15:11). Though there are times when the gifts and graces of God seem distant, joy can be the overall spirit of our lives.

The Apostle Paul wrote to the young churches of his day:

The fruit of the Spirit is . . . joy (Gal. 5:22). Do not get drunk with wine, for that is dissipation, but be filled with the Spirit, speaking to one another in psalms and hymns and spiritual songs, singing and making melody with your heart to the Lord (Eph. 5:18-19).

Christ Saves the Best for Last
The joy Jesus gives improves with age. When the headwaiter tasted the wine that Jesus produced, he said to the family, "Every man serves the good wine first, and when men have drunk freely, then that which is poorer; you have kept the good wine until now" (John 2:10). Though the natural wines of life tend to lose their sparkle as we get older, the wine that Christ gives—the joys we have in Him—increases with vitality. I have found that to be true—He is serving delicacies at my table now that I knew nothing of in my early years of Christian

experience. Jesus always gives something better than we have known before. Our tastes too should become more refined. The promise of joy is a promise of growth. In the words of the psalmist:

> The righteous man will flourish like the palm tree, he will grow like a cedar in Lebanon. Planted in the house of the Lord, they will flourish in the courts of our God. They will still yield fruit in old age; they shall be full of sap and very green (Ps. 92:12-14).

We all know some people like that. As they move into their later years, they become more joyous, more vigorous, and effervescent. This promise means that as we move into midlife and then into our more mature years, and finally old age, and on into eternity, we can anticipate a special kind of joy, for our Lord saves the best for last.

That Christ's first miracle was performed at a wedding speaks to us of another wedding yet to be, where Christ will be more than a guest. He will be the Bridegroom and the church will be the bride. The Apostle John wrote, "Blessed are those who are invited to the marriage supper of the Lamb" (Rev. 19:9).

The invitation to that supper, and the presence of joy in our lives now, are for people who have become part of God's family through Christ. To His bride, Christ gives "a garland instead of ashes, the oil of gladness instead of mourning" (Isa. 61:3).

Because Christ deals in joy and He keeps an open store, the invitation is still good:

> "Ho! Everyone who thirsts, come to the waters; And you who have no money come, buy and eat. Come, buy wine and milk without money and without cost" (Isa. 55:1).

5
Lion in the Temple

It was close to the time of Passover and there was a spirit of expectancy in Israel. Jewish tradition required an entire month of preparation for Passover. Roads were repaired, bridges rebuilt or shored up, and tombs whitewashed. The entire country bustled with the spirit of the holiday, and so we aren't surprised to read in the Gospel of John that Jesus went to Jerusalem to celebrate the feast.

Scholars estimate that more than two million people may have crowded into Jerusalem at Passover. As Jesus traveled south to Jerusalem, the roads must have been very congested. When He entered the gates of the city and approached the great cream and gold temple, He saw the sellers of trinkets and souvenirs on all sides.

This may have concerned Him, but not as much as what He saw when He stepped into the outer court of the temple. He found in the temple those who were selling oxen and sheep and doves, and the money changers seated (John 2:14).

The money changers claimed their business was a necessity. They had to change foreign currency into Jewish currency because foreign money was not acceptable as an offering in the temple. Authorities tell us that the money changers charged as much as two hours of a working man's wage to change a half shekel. They charged the same amount again for every half-shekel they gave in return for a larger coin. So if a man came in with a two-shekel piece, he would have to pay an entire day's wage just to change his money. The temple was taking in great sums of money. In fact, some years before, a man had ravaged the temple, taking the equivalent of $20 million, and hadn't come close to depleting the treasury of the temple.

All the sacrifices in the temple were peddled by the sellers and inspectors. Rabbinical literature tells us that inspectors spent eighteen months on a farm learning to distinguish between a clean and an unclean animal. They even learned to identify an animal that would one day become unclean! If the inspectors did not want to approve an animal, it could not be approved. Extortion was common in the temple confines, and it was said that Annas the high priest was behind the whole operation. Commentators of that day dubbed the temple "the bazaars of Annas." They knew the high priest sold franchises for the money-changing booths and for the stalls to sell animals.

An Angry Christ
When Jesus entered the temple, He found a religious circus. As He scanned the great court of the Gentiles, He saw sheep, oxen, fowl, and all the sounds and smells that go with them. He saw huckstering, bartering, and haggling over the weight of a coin. It was more than He could tolerate. Jesus reached down, picked up some cords, and quickly knotted them together. Above the din, He shouted, "Take these things away; stop making My Father's house a house of merchandise" (2:16).

His whip began to fly. Tables crashed, money jangled across the floor as Jesus drove the money changers, the sellers, and the inspectors out of the temple.

Gentle Jesus, meek and mild, is a concept so overworked that many preach and follow a Christ who has no resemblance to the

Christ of the New Testament. The Jesus they preach is an idol drained of His deity, a good-natured god whose great aim is to let us off the hook. It is people of this type who have suggested that Jesus twisted together a few reeds into the semblance of a scourge but did not use it.

It is true that Jesus described Himself as "meek and lowly in heart" (Matt. 11:29, KJV) and said, "Blessed are the meek; for they shall inherit the earth" (5:5, KJV). He displayed matchless humility under the infinite stress and humiliation of His passion and crucifixion. "Being reviled, He did not revile in return; while suffering, He uttered no threats" (1 Peter 2:23).

Yet to have a balanced picture of Jesus, we need to see Him in other settings, as on the day when He was about to heal the man with the withered hand. He looked around at all those who questioned His performing a miracle on the Sabbath and He was filled with a swelling wrath (Mark 3:5). There was nothing gentle in the message He sent to King Herod, "Go and tell that fox" (Luke 13:32), or in His response to Peter, "Get behind Me, Satan!" (Matt. 16:23) His reproach of the Pharisees was far from mild: "You are like whitewashed tombs" (23:27), or "You serpents, you brood of vipers, how shall you escape the sentence of hell?" (23:33)

As Christ lashed the whip at the money changers, He was as fully Godlike as when He stood on the Mount of Transfiguration or when He hung on the cross of Calvary. To understand His action in the temple, we need to look at the reason for His anger.

The Root of Christ's Anger

Christ's anger was directed at the irreverence of the Jews toward God the Father. The purpose of the temple was to glorify God. Years earlier, when Solomon finished building the temple and the people were gathered for its dedication, the ark of the covenant was placed in the temple. As the ark representing God's presence entered the temple, a thick cloud denoting

God's glory filled the temple. It was so dense that the priests could not work for a time.

While the religious authorities of Jesus' day loudly proclaimed the holiness and otherness of God, they denied it in practice. Our Lord's whip was loosed against what detracted from the communication of God's glory, especially in worship.

This has meaning for our own day. Many Christians have made valid attempts to present the humanity of Christ so that people can see Him as a God who relates to their lives. But this attitude has been carried to such extremes that for many people, Jesus has been emptied of His deity. It is easy to fall into such flippancy, and yet its result is a form of idolatry, a distortion of God into man-made images.

Such distortion is implicit when people refer to Him as "the big man in the sky." Even the very religious are not immune to devaluating God's divinity by emphasizing His humanity, as when a former Archbishop of Canterbury stood to his feet at the end of a performance of *Godspell* and shouted, "Long live God," which, as Malcolm Muggeridge observed, is like shouting, "Carry on eternity," or "Keep going infinity." What must God think of such a remark? We must be careful never to defame God by our irreverence, whatever the form. Irreverence brings God's anger (Malcolm Muggeridge, *The End of Christendom*, Eerdmans, p. 13).

Yet an even greater reason for Christ's anger was His love for God the Father. In Psalm 69 we read, "Zeal for Thy house has consumed me" (v. 9). In Greek, the word *consume* means to be eaten up by. The Hebrew word for consume means "to burn up." The Psalm is about David, but has its prophetic fulfillment in Christ. Jesus was aflame with zeal for God's glory and for His house.

The full meaning of this saying can be seen in the second half of Psalm 69:9: "And the reproaches of those who reproach Thee have fallen on me." What David meant was that if someone defamed God, he too was defamed. Christ would have felt this even more keenly than David. What a wonderful possibility for us to be so identified with God that when His name is defamed, we feel it and experience holy anger.

It is a pity that we have been so tamed by our culture. We have bought into the fallacy that thoughtful and intelligent people should discuss even the most outrageous matters without emotion. John Ruskin, speaking of his own time, in his *Lectures on Art,* said, "I believe it to be quite one of the crowning wickednesses of this age that we have starved and chilled our faculty of indignation" (quoted by C. J. Wright, *Jesus the Revelation of God,* Hodder and Stoughton, p. 44).

In His anger Jesus was revealing a great truth—that love presupposes hatred. A love for the downtrodden, the poor, and the oppressed is accompanied by a hatred for the conditions that cause the suffering. This truth was evidenced in the lives of the Earl of Shaftsbury who helped alleviate the terrible labor conditions spawned by the Industrial Revolution, of Elizabeth Fry who did so much to bring prison reform, and of John Woolman in his stand against slavery.

We can tell as much about a person by what he hates as by his loves. We should be passionate people, angered by what angers Christ.

Need for Reverence

If we understand who God is, we live and worship with reverence. If we do not know God as He is, an irreverent spirit takes root and intrudes on our ability to worship. While we are sitting in church, our hearts may be like that outer court of the temple, full of disorder, greed, irreverence. Solomon expressed it this way, "I was almost in utter ruin in the midst of the assembly and congregation" (Prov. 5:14). It is possible to be in church, ostensibly at worship, yet almost in utter ruin.

In his wonderful book, *The Knowledge of the Holy,* the late A. W. Tozer explained how this happens:

With our loss of the sense of majesty has come the further loss of religious awe and consciousness of the divine presence. We have lost our spirit of worship and our ability to withdraw inwardly to meet God in adoring silence. Modern Christianity is simply not producing the kind of Christian who can appreciate or experience the life in the Spirit. The words, "Be still, and know that I am God," mean next to nothing to the self-confident, bustling worshiper in this middle period of the twentieth century (Harper and Row, p. 6).

A person who has an irreverent spirit and an idolatrous concept of God will carry these into his attempts to serve God. The profit motive, so evident in the temple, moves right into the church of our day. The person who sees God as impotent, effete, or obsolete will feel the need to help Him by introducing objectives and methods which actually defame Him.

The degree of our reverence indicates what we think of God. Irreverence is a symptom of an idolatrous concept of God, a man-made god. Reverence for God indicates our belief that He is great, awesome, and powerful.

We live in a narcissistic, individualistic society that encourages us to go our own ways. The body of Christ is not to function this way. We need each other, in fellowship, in teaching, in worship. It is wonderful to worship with God's people, for joyful worship makes known the living God. A joyless ritual, on the other hand, suggests that God is far away or dead.

After Jesus had cleansed the temple, His detractors approached Him with a question:

"What sign do You show to us, seeing that You do these things?" Jesus answered and said to them, "Destroy this temple, and in three days I will raise it up." The Jews therefore said, "It took forty-six years to build this temple, and will You raise it up in three days?" But He was speaking of the temple of His body (John 2:18-21).

While Christ was speaking about His resurrection in which He would be gloriously vindicated, His words had another meaning. As no other person, our Lord was the temple of God. We read of Christ, "For in Him all the fullness of deity dwells in bodily form" (Col. 2:9).

What Kind of Temple?
Before He returned to heaven, He promised His followers that they would receive the Holy Spirit to be with and in them always. He was promising that they would be the temple of God.

For we are the temple of the living God; just as God said, "I will dwell in them and walk among them; and I will be their God, and they shall be My people" (2 Cor. 6:16).

When we think that God dwells in us, the cleansing of the temple has personal meaning. Are our lives filled with the Shekinah glory, like the holy of holies? Or are they more like banks? Playhouses? Recreational vehicles? Libraries? Sties of sensuality?

Jesus cares about His temples and comes with whip in hand when necessary. He cleansed the temple in Jerusalem more than once. And He comes again and again to our lives to cleanse us, if we are not glorifying Him.

When He comes, we should praise Him for His correcting whip and His anger toward the sin in our lives. Then with the psalmist we can say, "Before I was afflicted I went astray, but now I keep Thy Word. It is good for me that I was afflicted" (Ps. 119:67, 71).

6

The Nonnegotiables of Salvation

It was during the presidential campaign of 1976 that Jimmy Carter told the nation he had been born again. I was driving along listening to the radio when I heard him say it. I gripped the steering wheel more firmly and said to myself, "How about that!"

In the years since, we have had born-again athletes, born-again porn, born-again companies, born-again buildings. A recent publication included a letter to the editor from a woman who claimed that she was a born-again Christian. She explained that along with being born again she had experienced an increased capacity to love, and that she and her husband were now expressing sexually their love to others, specifically to their pastor and his wife! Along similar lines, a young woman claims that she is "stripping for Jesus." Her rationale is that since the Lord gave her a beautiful body, stripping is the best way to use her gift!

When a phrase becomes part of the common parlance, it is easy for us to forget its real meaning. Yet this expression is one that we dare not ignore or lose, because being born again is essential to being a Christian.

A wise and good man of Jesus' time wasn't sure what Jesus meant when He said that a person had to be born again. In that, he was like many people today. As we listen in on the conversation between Jesus and Nicodemus, our understanding of this essential to salvation will increase.

Seeking Truth

"Now there was a man of the Pharisees, named Nicodemus, a ruler of the Jews" (John 3:1).

Whatever else we think of the Pharisees, we have to admit they were earnest. They were so serious about their faith that on the Sabbath they would carry no more food than the weight of a dried fig, and no more milk than could be swallowed in one gulp, lest they break the Sabbath rest. They were so fastidious about the observance of the Sabbath laws that they limited the number of nails in their sandals so they would not carry a burden on the Holy Day.

At times their seriousness led them into ridiculous situations. For instance, it was determined that on the Sabbath one could not tie a knot in a rope, but that a woman could tie a knot in her sash. So, if a man needed to draw water out of a well on the Sabbath, and nothing was already tied to the bucket, he could tie his wife's sash to the handle.

The Pharisees were desperately fervent. Nicodemus was not playing games in his religious experience. He was a member of the Sanhedrin, a group of seventy men, lay and clerical, who had jurisdiction over Jews in all parts of the world. In addition, he was a teacher of the Jews. It is believed that he was among the greatest of teachers, and there is contemporary evidence that he came from an aristocratic family that traced back to the Maccabees.

Nicodemus was a highly educated man and an aristocrat. He was a ruler, a teacher, and a seeker after truth. All of this, coupled with the fact that he ultimately did respond to Christ (7:50-52; 19:39-40) makes his life a perfect setting in which to discover the essentials of the born-again experience.

On a quiet Palestinian evening, a perplexed man moved along the serpentine back streets of Old Jerusalem to talk with a young Rabbi. It was to be the greatest meeting of his life:

> This man came to Him by night, and said to Him, "Rabbi, we know that You have come from God as a teacher; for no one can do these signs that You do unless God is with him." Jesus answered and said to him, "Truly, truly, I say to you, unless one is born again, he cannot see the kingdom of God" (3:2-3).

Nicodemus approached Jesus respectfully, using the honored title "Rabbi." He was prepared for an exchange of philosophical ideas, but certainly not for the conversation that followed. With what might seem rudeness, Jesus cut him off and went straight to the heart of the matter. In that moment, the vocabulary of faith was given one of its greatest expressions—*born again*.

It has been a bad habit of most expositors to portray Nicodemus as stupid in his response to Jesus. However, we must realize that Jesus never would have expressed such an esoteric concept to a theologically ignorant person. Nicodemus understood what *born again* meant within his own religious context. The rabbis had a saying, "A proselyte who embraces Judaism is like a newborn child." They even theorized that when a man entered into Judaism, he was such a new man he could marry his mother or sister! All things were to be completely new, all old connections destroyed. So when Nicodemus heard Jesus say that he needed to be born again, he understood what that would mean for a convert to Judaism. But he *was* a Jew, a teacher, a member of the Sanhedrin. What did it mean for him?

> Nicodemus said to Him, "How can a man be born when he is old? He cannot enter a second time into his mother's womb and be born, can he?" (3:4)

Nicodemus was not naively suggesting some sort of gynecological miracle. Rather, it was with wistful yearning that he said, "You talk about being born again. You talk about that radical, fundamental change which is necessary. I know it is necessary, but I question how it happens. There is nothing I would like more. But you might as well tell me that I, as a full-grown man, need to reenter my mother's womb and be born all over again. I long for the new birth. But how?"

Alfred Lord Tennyson portrayed this thought in his poem "Maud."

> And oh for a man to rise in me,
> That the man that I am may cease to be!

This is the heart cry of mankind. We desire to change. We want to be different. We need new minds and new personalities. We want to be born again, but how? It is as difficult as reentering the womb but it can really happen.

Jesus answered, "Truly, truly, I say to you, unless one is born of water and the Spirit, he cannot enter into the kingdom of God" (v. 5).

Nicodemus knew something of what Jesus meant. He knew that John the Baptist was baptizing men in water as a symbol of their inward repentance (3:23). Nicodemus may have thought, "Except you are born of all that water baptism signifies, which is repentance, and that which Spirit baptism accomplishes, which is regeneration, you cannot enter the kingdom of God." Nicodemus probably saw very clearly that no one is truly born again if there is not repentance, and that along with repentance comes a work of the Spirit in the heart. These are the nonnegotiables of being born again—repentance and a work of God in the heart. This brings us to a problem of our day.

Repentance

In the years following President Carter's declaration that he had been born again, there was high interest in the U.S. in finding out how many of his fellow Americans also claimed this experience. A 1979 Gallup Poll reported that nearly 40 million Americans said they had asked Christ to be their Saviour. One in five adults, about 31 million, considered themselves evangelicals.

After these statistics were made public, serious questions were asked. If the numbers are true, why is the pace of sin accelerating? Why is pornography on the upswing? Why is personal and corporate immorality epidemic?

The questions continue today and succeeding polls have brought to light some answers which, if not surprising, are disturbing. Incredible ignorance of Christ exists in the church. Of those who claim to be evangelicals, three in ten do not think the devil is a personal being. Only six in ten can correctly identify "You must be born again" as words which Jesus spoke.

With this kind of ignorance, it follows that the moral and ethical teachings contained in the Scripture are even less understood. It is possible that a new Christian may improperly repent, because of a lack of knowledge of right or wrong. One convert, three months after she became a Christian, gave her father a Playboy calendar for his birthday. It never occurred to her that such a gift would be contrary to the Christian life. Such happenings are commonplace because people in the church have not been adequately instructed, and because society no longer takes its norms from the Judeo-Christian ethic.

Another, and far more important, reason for discrepancy between profession and action is that many people who say they are born again know nothing of repentance. This means that multiplied thousands who claim to be Christians really are not. Jesus said that unless a person is born of water—repentance— it is impossible to enter the kingdom of God.

What does repentance mean? Something that happened to a

college boy illustrates it well. He was a football player, and on his team, chewing tobacco was the "in" thing. One night after practice, this boy went up to another player's room, bit off a big chew and slipped it into the back of his mouth. By mistake he swallowed a bit and it burned. In his confusion he swallowed even more, and he began to be very sick. He could barely make his way out of the room and down the stairs. When he got outside, everything came up. He was so sick that he lay on the pavement on his back and watched the moons—all three of them—whirling around. That night he repented. He hasn't had a chew since.

Not only did he repent, but he changed his mind. The Greek word for repentance comes from the coupling of two words, one meaning "after" and the other meaning "thought" or "mind." Together they mean "to rethink" or "to change one's mind." Chewing tobacco no longer occupied that boy's mind. It was repugnant to him.

With repentance comes a change of action corresponding to the change of mind. Repentance is not simply taking a new direction or turning around. It is not education. It is not a religious rite for which a church can set the stage.

Being born again is not "asking Jesus into your heart." If you ask Him into your heart, without having repented, you will not be regenerated. Being born again is a radical change that takes place. Through the work of the Spirit which enables repentance, you are given a new nature:

> Therefore, if any man is in Christ, he is a new creature; the old things passed away; behold, new things have come (2 Cor. 5:17).

The Work of the Holy Spirit
Our Lord further explains this radical change:

> That which is born of the flesh is flesh; and that which is born of the Spirit is spirit. Do not marvel that I said to you, "You must be born again" (John 3:6-7).

The radical change is not something which can be accomplished by human energy. The Apostle Peter described it as our being made partakers of the divine nature (2 Peter 1:4).

There is a story of an Arabian Chicken Little, actually a sparrow, who had heard that the sky was falling. An Arab saw the bird lying on its back with its scrawny legs thrust upward. On inquiring if the bird was all right and why it was in such a position, the sparrow explained that he was doing his part to keep the sky from falling. The Arab asked, "You surely don't think you are going to hold it up with those scrawny legs, do you?"

With a solemn look at the Arab, the sparrow retorted, "One does the best one can."

Our best will never suffice for us to be born again. This is the point of Jesus' words: "That which is born of the flesh is flesh and that which is born of the Spirit is spirit." Vegetable stays vegetable. Flesh remains flesh. There is no evolution from flesh to spirit.

To be born again, we must realize that we are sinners, repent, and receive the work of the Spirit in our lives. The question is not whether we have had a religious experience; rather whether we have been born again.

While Jesus and Nicodemus were talking, they may have heard the wind moaning along the narrow streets. Possibly it stirred the leaves that overhung the window casements and then entered the room with an evening breeze. As Jesus said to Nicodemus:

> The wind blows where it wishes and you hear the sound of it, but do not know where it comes from and where it is going; so is everyone who is born of the Spirit (v. 8).

Jesus was saying, "Nicodemus, being born of the Spirit is like your experience with the wind."

When we are born again, the effects of the Spirit are visible in our lives, even though the Spirit is not seen. Sometimes the Spirit is forceful, other times gentle.

Is the Spirit in your life—perhaps gently soothing your soul, assuring you that you have been born again?

Or, the Spirit may be convicting you, and for the first time you are seeing the nonnegotiables of salvation. You may be seeing your sin and realizing your need to repent. You desire the Spirit to make you a new person.

> As many as received Him, to them He gave the right to become children of God, even to those who believe in His name: who were born not of blood, nor of the will of the flesh, nor of the will of man, but of God (1:12-13).

If the Holy Spirit is speaking to you, why not pray? As you pray,

• Confess your sins and thank Christ for dying on the cross to atone for them. Affirm that you are trusting Him alone for your salvation.

• Affirm that you are repenting (turning) from your sin.

• Ask Christ to make you a new person by the power of the Holy Spirit.

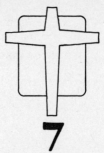

7
The Meaning of
the Cross

A radical change takes place when a person is born again. We can see the results, just as we see the effects of the wind. A near hurricane may bend the shrubbery and uproot tall trees, while a breeze imperceptibly touches a leaf. So the Spirit touches lives, sometimes with upheaval, sometimes with gentleness. However it is experienced, when a person is really born again, a radical work of the Spirit takes place.

When Jesus explained this spiritual dynamic to Nicodemus, the great teacher of Israel, Nicodemus asked, "How can these things be?" (John 3:9)

Jesus' reply, while a mild rebuke to Nicodemus, centers on Jesus' authority, not only to answer the question but to be the answer:

Jesus answered and said to him, "Are you the teacher of Israel, and do not understand these things? Truly, truly, I say to you, we speak that which we know, and bear witness of that which we have seen; and you do not receive our witness.

"If I told you earthly things and you do not believe, how shall you believe if I tell you heavenly things? And no one has ascended

into heaven, but He who descended from heaven, even the Son
of man.

"And as Moses lifted up the serpent in the wilderness, even
so must the Son of man be lifted up; that whoever believes may
in Him have eternal life" (vv. 10-15).

Nicodemus knew the history of his people. Jesus was reminding him of an incident that happened to the Children of Israel
during the forty years they wandered in the wilderness near
Sinai, the mountain of God, by way of the Red Sea, to go around
the land of Edom. When we consider that traveling meant taking with them everything they owned—household goods, animals, personal effects, and tents—we can understand how they
became impatient and out of sorts. When things go wrong, it
is easy to blame the leader, but they carried it too far. They
spoke against both Moses and God as they said, "Why have you
brought us up out of Egypt to die in the wilderness? For there
is no food and no water, and we loathe this miserable food"
(Num. 21:5).

The Lord was so displeased with the people that He sent a
punishment on them. Poisonous serpents bit them and many
died. The people came to Moses and confessed that they had
sinned in speaking against him and the Lord, and begged Moses
to intercede with God to remove the serpents. After Moses
prayed, God said to him:

"Make a fiery serpent and set it on a standard; and it shall come
about, that everyone who is bitten, when he looks at it, he shall
live." And Moses made a bronze serpent, and set it on the
standard; and it came about, that if a serpent bit any man, when
he looked to the bronze serpent, he lived (Num. 21:8-9).

Provision for Healing

The picture Jesus brought to the mind of Nicodemus was one
of both horror and glory. It was horrible that the Israelites were
beset by venomous snakes that left them dead or inflamed with

fever. And yet in this picture we see God's provision for heal-ing. In speaking of this event, Jesus left no doubt about the application: Jesus, the Son of man, would be raised up high on a pole to become the cure for the poison of sin that was killing the people.

The symbolism is remarkable: a serpent is a figure of sin, a serpent tempted Adam and Eve in the garden, thereby bringing sin into the world, and human nature is infected. When Paul spoke about the human condition, he said, "There is none righ-teous, not even one" (Rom. 3:10).

It is significant that Moses used the likeness of a serpent, rather than an actual one. When our Lord became the sacrifice for our sins, He too assumed the likeness of a serpent. The Scriptures say that God sent "His own Son in the likeness of sinful flesh and as an offering for sin" (Rom. 8:3). "He made Him who knew no sin to be sin on our behalf, that we might become the righteousness of God in Him" (2 Cor. 5:21). "Christ redeemed us from the curse of the Law, having become a curse for us" (Gal. 3:13). Christ became what He was not: a curse, sin, so that He might take away our sin.

The second parallel in the two events centers on the look of faith. When the Children of Israel looked on the bronze serpent, they lived. No matter how horribly the Israelites were bitten and infected, no matter how many times they had been bitten, they had the chance to be saved by looking at the serpent. The command to look to that uplifted serpent was a gracious fore-shadowing of our looking to Christ for our salvation. And be-cause Christ was lifted up on the cross, even the most degraded and miserable sinner who looks to Him will be saved.

Though Nicodemus probably didn't understand completely what Jesus meant when He said, "The Son of man must be lifted up," he knew the significance of the illustration from the Book of Numbers. Later, when Jesus was crucified, Nicodemus was able to put it together quickly. It was he, along with Joseph of Arimathea, who buried Jesus' body (John 19:38-40).

How does the new birth happen? Jesus pointed to the Atonement. He answered in a way that Nicodemus would never forget. The radical change of the new birth is possible only when Christ takes our infected (sinful) natures on Himself, bears the venom, and imparts new natures to us: "If any man is in Christ, he is a new creature; the old things passed away; behold, new things have come" (2 Cor. 5:17).

Looking to the Cross

We are saved by the simple look of faith, not a perfect work of faith. Some think they cannot come to Jesus till they have enough faith. If the dying Israelites had waited for perfect faith, more of them would have died. Some must have cherished doubts and procrastinated. Not all had the same quality of faith, but they looked to the serpent.

We are to look to the Cross. A sinner who has a repentant spirit, and who knows that Jesus Christ bore his sins on the cross, can look to Him and be saved.

God's Love Manifested

Jesus followed His illustration of the serpent with the greatest of explanations:

> For God so loved the world, that He gave His only begotten Son, that whoever believes in Him should not perish, but have eternal life (John 3:16).

Martin Luther called this verse "the Gospel in miniature." D.L. Moody claimed that this verse brought him to an understanding of the love of God. Early in his ministry, he went to England. While there, he met Henry Morehouse, a young minister. When Morehouse said that he was thinking of going to America, Moody responded, "Well, if you should ever get to Chicago, come down to my church and I will give you a chance to preach." Moody had not heard Morehouse preach, and after he made his offer, he hoped the man would never come.

After Moody was back in Chicago, he received a telegram which read, "Just arrived in New York. Will be in Chicago on Sunday. Morehouse." Moody was in a quandary. He had to be out of town the next Sunday. He had promised the man his pulpit, but had never heard him preach. After discussing the matter with his best counselor, his wife, and also with the church leaders, Moody decided to allow Morehouse to preach once. If that sermon was acceptable, he could preach again. And so Moody left Chicago and Morehouse arrived.

At the end of the week, Moody returned home and asked his wife, "How did the young preacher do?"

She answered, "He is a better preacher than you are. He is telling sinners that God loves them. You must hear Him!"

"What? He is telling sinners that God loves them? That's not true!"

"Well," she said, "He has been preaching on John 3:16 all week long."

That night Moody heard Morehouse say, "I have been hunting for a text and I have not been able to find a better one than John 3:16, so I will talk about it once more." That night Moody saw the greatness of God's love in a way he never had before (James M. Boice, *The Gospel of John*, Vol. 1, Zondervan, pp. 279-280).

It is not simply that God is love, but that "God so loved that He gave." This is what makes the new birth possible. For God's love effects a result: "that whoever believes in Him should not perish but have eternal life." When we believe, we gain eternal life as our present possession. When we die, we shall be even more alive than we are now.

This life is offered to the world, the *cosmos*, a word used 186 times in the Greek New Testament and always in connection with the idea of sin. God loves a sinful world. To gain eternal life we must believe in Christ. "Whoever believes may in Him have eternal life" and "He who believes in Him is not judged" (3:15, 18).

God	The greatest lover
so loved	The greatest degree
the world	The greatest company
that He gave	The greatest act
His only Son	The greatest gift
that whosoever	The greatest opportunity
believeth	The greatest simplicity
in Him	The greatest attraction
should not perish	The greatest promise
but	The greatest difference
have	The greatest certainty
everlasting life	The greatest possession

"For God did not send the Son into the world to judge the world; but that the world should be saved through Him. He who believes in Him is not judged; he who does not believe has been judged already, because he has not believed in the name of the only begotten Son of God" (3:17-18).

Responding to the Light

Christ did not come into the world to judge the world, but judgment comes through Him, nonetheless. Because of this, there is constant conflict between good and evil, light and darkness. How a person responds to the light is indicative of his response to the new birth offered by Christ:

"And this is the judgment, that the light is come into the world, and men loved the darkness rather than the light; for their deeds were evil. For everyone who does evil hates the light, and does not come to the light, lest his deeds should be exposed. But he who practices the truth comes to the light, that his deeds may be manifested as having been wrought in God" (3:19-21).

The illustration of the serpent lifted up is helpful because it not only reveals the solution for sin, but also tells us that the solution is not self-betterment or self-healing. Man's remedies will not work.

Dr. Donald Grey Barnhouse emphasized this, suggesting that the Children of Israel could have mobilized to fight the deadly serpents. They could have incorporated a Society for the Extermination of Fiery Serpents. They could have worn badges, given membership cards, elected officers, held rallies, issued photographs of slain serpents to the press, and played down the statistics of death. They even could have made offerings to the serpents. But it would have been to no avail. (Donald Grey Barnhouse, *God's Remedy*, Scripture Truth, Vol. 2, p. 221).

None of our efforts to save ourselves work. Rather, we must give up dependence on ourselves—our cleverness, our self-improvements, our intelligence, our religious ceremonies, and our natural gifts—and look to Christ.

The new nature comes through the atonement of Christ who was lifted up so that He might draw all men to Himself. Before His death, He said, "And I, if I be lifted up from the earth, will draw all men to Myself" (12:32).

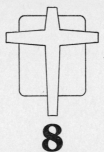

8
Resisting Jealousy

No matter who we are, or what degree of success we have known, sooner or later our lives or our work will be eclipsed by someone else. The most competent of us will someday be surpassed, and we need to know how to react to this.

A regrettable competition exists among Christians. It is not new, for the Bible recounts instances of it. When the Apostle Paul was under house arrest in Philippi, some of his competitors were making the most of the new attention given to them. Paul's reaction to this?

> Some, to be sure, are preaching Christ even from envy and strife, but some also from good will; the latter do it out of love, knowing that I am appointed for the defense of the Gospel; the former proclaim Christ out of selfish ambition, rather than from pure motives, thinking to cause me distress in my imprisonment (Phil. 1:15-17).

Some were preaching the Gospel out of selfish ambition, Paul said. The word translated "ambition" is one which means political ambition. We see this type of competitiveness in the church.

Years ago I heard Dr. Kenneth Chapin, pastor of the Main Street Baptist Church of Houston, tell about a test he gave his students when he was teaching in seminary. This test was a scientifically designed word association to show the students how they related ideas. The teacher mentioned a word and the students wrote what first came to mind.

Dr. Chapin was appalled to find the degree of bitterness, resentment, and prejudice in those men preparing for the ministry. Words such as *truck driver* invariably brought such derogatory responses as *lazy*. Through the test and subsequent conversations, he came to realize that people who go into the ministry are often negative and highly competitive. Some of them particularly dislike preachers!

The pervasiveness of this phenomena throughout church history produced a cynical Latin phrase—*odium theologicum* meaning "the hatred of theologians." Few sins give the enemies of Christianity more occasion for blasphemy than a jealous spirit among Christian leaders.

John's Eclipse

In John 3, we have an illustration of a competent man being eclipsed by another. While John the Baptist continued to preach and baptize in the wilderness, Jesus also began preaching and baptizing. Two groups were administering the baptism of repentance, though Jesus did not personally baptize people (4:2).

When the disciples of John saw that Jesus was overshadowing their leader, they were jealous for John. The conflict surfaced during a discussion between John's disciples and a Jew about the rite of purification. While we don't know the details of that conversation, it seems that the Jewish detractor asked, "Well, which baptism is superior, Jesus' or John's?"

Confusion rose among John's disciples and they came to him asking, "Rabbi, He who was with you beyond the Jordan, to whom you have borne witness, behold, He is baptizing, and all are coming to Him" (3:26).

While it was hardly true that all the people were following Jesus, it was true that John's disciples saw their leader's star sinking. They saw his ministry diminishing and wondered what they should do. They didn't want John to take a backseat.

It was all very human. To watch the ebbing of a ministry is disappointing. John's disciples saw people turning away from their leader and they resented the disloyalty. They thought that Jesus' success was in part due to the testimony of John.

It must also have been a temptation to John the Baptist to feel resentful and jealous. He had spent many years of loneliness and self-denial in the wilderness. He understood alienation from his culture for the sake of his ministry. It would have been easy for John to yield to a natural impulse to assert himself.

Because the temptation is the same today, we need to look at John's responses to see what kept him from bitterness.

John's Philosophy
John stood before his angry and excited disciples and quietly answered their resentful assertions with a proverb: "A man can receive nothing, unless it has been given him from heaven" (3:27). That means that if a man is displaying gifts superior to yours and having greater success, it is because God has given it to him. This is the proper philosophy by which to evaluate the successes of others.

It is also the way to evaluate our own successes. We tend to play down the successes of others and uplift our own. If another person is doing quite well, we attribute it to a "silver spoon" or "being in the right place at the right time." But when we happen to be especially successful, we think it is because of our prowess, intelligence, and hard work!

The Apostle Paul wrote to the church at Corinth:

What are you so puffed up about? What do you have that God hasn't given you? And if all you have is from God, why act as though you are so great, and as though you have accomplished something on your own? (1 Cor. 4:7, TLB)

Whether we are looking at ourselves or others, the proper way to evaluate success is to remember that we can receive nothing unless it has been given from heaven.

John the Baptist held a high view of God as the sovereign bestower of gifts. He could tolerate being outstripped by another because he knew that God does not make mistakes. How liberating when this is a reality in our lives. I have seen this truth literally revolutionize people. When they saw that God had sovereignly given them the gifts, abilities, and talents they have, they became free.

John's words reflect his overwhelming desire for God's glory. John the Baptist applied his philosophy to his own life: "You yourselves bear me witness, that I said, 'I am not the Christ,' but, 'I have been sent before Him' " (John 3:28).

John knew who he was. He had a good self-image. He knew that God had appointed the differences between him and the One who outshone him, the One he was free to serve with no tinge of rivalry, jealousy, insecurity, or bitterness. John kept right on ministering, even though Jesus was a few miles away, drawing larger crowds and greater public acclaim.

Do you feel outdone? Outclassed? Eclipsed? Has someone come into your life who is obviously more gifted or more effective than you are? Adopt the philosophy of John the Baptist: "A man can receive nothing, unless it is given to him from heaven." When this principle operates in your life, you will experience security, joy in God's work, humility, and freedom.

John's Attitude

"He who has the bride is the bridegroom; but the friend of the bridegroom, who stands and hears him, rejoices greatly because of the bridegroom's voice. And so this joy of mine has been made full" (3:29).

John expressed his feelings about the ministry of Christ in a superbly rich metaphor, as he compared himself to the friend of the bridegroom in a Hebrew wedding. William Barclay wrote:

The "friend of the bridegroom," the *shoshben,* had a unique place at a Jewish wedding. He acted as the liaison between the bride and the bridegroom; he arranged the wedding; he took out the invitations; he presided at the wedding feast. He brought the bride and the bridegroom together. And he had one special duty. It was his duty to guard the bridal chamber and to let no false lover in. He would only open the door when in the dark he heard the bridegroom's voice and recognized it. When he heard the bridegroom's voice he was glad and he let him in, and he went away rejoicing, for his task was completed (*The Gospel of John,* Westminster, Vol. 1, pp. 134-135).

John claimed that he found fullness of joy in his Master's voice. This is the preeminent application for us today. We are to find our joy in Christ, not only as His friend but also as His bride, the church.

John's use of this illustration suggests that when others outstrip us we are to share in the joy of their accomplishments, just as the best man shared the joy of the bridegroom.

I remember what a great event it was when I was best man for my closest friend, David MacDonald. We had been friends since we were teenagers, had gotten into trouble together, had double-dated together, and were college roommates. Dave offered me a wonderful gift when he asked me to be best man. As I stood next to him during the ceremony, I wasn't jealous. I didn't want to be in his place. Though his bride was beautiful, I did not begrudge him. Rather, my joy was intimately tied to his joy. His happiness was my happiness.

As members of the church, the body of Christ, we should rejoice in one another's successes. The Apostle Paul wrote about this sharing: "And if one member suffers, all the members suffer with it; if one member is honored, all the members rejoice with it" (1 Cor. 12:26).

Because John the Baptist could so thoroughly enter into the ministry of Christ and rejoice in it, even though it took away from his following, Christ commended him: "Truly, I say to you, among those born of women there has not arisen anyone greater than John the Baptist" (Matt. 11:11).

John's humility was the key to his greatness, just as was true with Moses. And this is the key to any greatness of ours, whether we serve in a large or small place.

John's Conduct

"He must increase, but I must decrease" (John 3:30).

When William Carey, the founder of modern missions, was dying, he turned to a friend and said, "When I am gone, don't talk about William Carey; talk about William Carey's Saviour. I desire that Christ alone might be magnified" (H.A. Ironside, *Addresses on the Gospel of John*, Loizeaux, pp. 126-127). That was the spirit of John the Baptist.

As a young preacher, F.B. Meyer ministered in London at the same time Charles Spurgeon was preaching in the great Metropolitan Tabernacle. Sunday after Sunday Meyer would stand on the steps of his church and watch the carriages go past enroute to Spurgeon's tabernacle. It was difficult for him to accept, but he did.

Toward the end of Meyer's life, when he was preaching in Northfield at the invitation of D.L. Moody, G. Campbell Morgan was also there preaching. Larger crowds came to hear Morgan than to hear Meyer. Meyer was not in his prime anymore, and Morgan was at his best. One day Meyer returned to his cottage feeling very sad about his seeming lack of success, and he went to the Lord in prayer. The next day Meyer went about Northfield asking people, "Have you heard Campbell Morgan preach? Did you hear his message this morning? My, but God is upon that man!"

This is the proper conduct for Christians. Are you envious of someone? A person whose success you secretly begrudge? Covenant before God to say something good to the person you envy, or speak well on his behalf. Pray for that person. William Law claimed it is impossible to harbor animosity and jealousy toward a person for whom you are praying:

When therefore you have once habituated your heart to a serious performance of this holy intercession, you have done a great deal to render it incapable of spite and envy, and to make it naturally to delight in the happiness of all mankind (*A Serious Call to Devout and Holy Life,* Wyvern Books, p. 212).

9

The Ministering Heart

We who claim the name of Christ have two distinct options. One is to cultivate a small heart. If our ambition is to avoid troubles and sorrows we should hold back from entangling relationships, and forget about noble ideals. That is the safest way.

The other option is to open ourselves to others, to become susceptible to the gamut of sorrows about which a shriveled heart knows nothing.

A sentence in the diary of James Gilmour, pioneer missionary to Mongolia, must have been written in blood. The words were penned late in Gilmour's life, after many years of missionary work: "In the shape of converts, I have seen no results. I have not, as far as I am aware, seen anyone who even wanted to be a Christian" (Clyde E. Fant, Jr. and William M. Pinson, Jr. eds. *Twenty Centuries of Great Preaching,* Word, Vol. 8, p. 76).

These painful words would never have been written if James Gilmour had not decided to go for it all and give his life in service to Christ. If he had never set out for Mongolia, he would not have found himself in this position of apparent failure and deep disappointment.

When we enlarge our hearts, and cultivate ministering

spirits, we increase potential for pain. You may have already experienced this kind of hurt because of deep commitment on your part. You pursued high ideals, you gave yourself to others, and your vulnerability left you prey to sorrows that you could have avoided had you not opened your heart.

Little hearts, though they seem safe and protected, never contribute. No one benefits from their restricted sympathies and limited vision. Ministering hearts, while vulnerable, know the most joy. They leave their imprint on the world.

The choice is ours. Cultivate deafness, and we will never hear the discords of life, but neither will we hear the glorious strains of a great symphony. Cultivate blindness, and we will never see the ugly, but neither will we see the beauty of God's creation. Cultivate a small heart and sailing may be smooth, but we will not know the "heady winds"—the Holy Spirit working. We will not see lives change.

We have only to read our newspapers to know the need for ministering, caring hearts. If, in response to need, you are feeling those strange and terrifying stirrings of soul, if you are facing the decision of whether to open your heart or close it, the story of our Lord and the woman at the well may be for you.

Ministering When Tired

He left Judea, and departed again into Galilee. And He had to pass through Samaria. So He came to a city of Samaria, called Sychar, near the parcel of ground that Jacob gave to his son Joseph; and Jacob's well was there. Jesus therefore, being wearied from His journey, was sitting thus by the well. It was about the sixth hour (John 4:3-6).

As Jesus and His disciples journeyed northward, they came to Jacob's well near Sychar. Because it was noontime, the disciples went into town to buy food while Jesus sat by the well. He reacted as any exhausted man would, and dropped down to rest.

The phrase "was sitting thus" (v.6) indicates that He sat down just as He was, like a tired man collapses after a hard day's work.

As we read the Gospels, we see that Jesus could hardly find two minutes to put together. He had to steal away to avoid the press of people. The multitudes wanted His help. The disciples constantly asked Him questions, and He needed to minister to them. He surely experienced mental and physical weariness.

Jesus may have closed His eyes as He reclined by the well, but when He heard approaching footsteps He looked up and saw the Samaritan woman. It would have been so easy for Him to rationalize, "I have been ministering to hundreds, and I am tired. I am a Jew and she is a Samaritan. I am a man and she is a woman. There are plenty of reasons not to talk to her. I need to relax."

That option was open to Jesus, but He didn't take it. He chose to minister to the heart of this woman even though He was near exhaustion.

A ministering heart carries on when it is at the edge of its capacity. Oswald Sanders wrote, "The world is run by tired men" (*Spiritual Leadership,* Moody Press, p. 108). Notwithstanding the fact that we need to take care of ourselves, I believe this is true. Author Ann Ortlund noted, "Nowhere in the Bible are we told to slow down and take it easy." We are to press on. We are not to be weary in well-doing. We are to run the good race. Rest and recreation must not be priorities.

Most souls are won for Christ by tired people.

The best sermons are preached by tired men.

The best camps are run by exhausted youth ministers.

The world is being evangelized by tired missionaries.

Christian organizations are being run by tired people.

The best Vacation Bible Schools are taught by tired women.

"Playing hurt" is an expression in the sports world. An athlete who endures and achieves his potential is one who learns to play with injuries. While I am not advocating playing while physically injured, in spiritual realities we need to learn to carry on when we don't feel like it. It has been my experience that the times I have been most used, I was at the point of exhaustion. We will never do great things for God until we learn to minister when we have tired hearts.

The Apostle Paul wrote of his own ministry: "For you recall, brethren, our labor and hardship, how working night and day so as not to be a burden to any of you, we proclaimed to you the Gospel of God" (1 Thes. 2:9).

Paul constantly worked to proclaim the Gospel. When he presented his credentials to the Corinthian church, he talked about the 195 lashes he had received, about the shipwrecks, the stonings, and the dangers he had endured (2 Cor. 11). What amazes me the most are these words:

> Apart from such external things, there is the daily pressure on me of concern for all the churches. Who is weak, without my being weak? Who is led into sin without my intense concern? (2 Cor. 11:28-29)

Paul gave his all in the service of Christ.

Martin Luther said he worked so hard that at night he literally fell into bed. In one account of his life, it says he did not change his bed for a year. Now that is being tired!

D.L. Moody's bedtime prayer on one occasion was, "Lord, I am tired. Amen." Calvin's biographers marveled at his output. John Wesley rode sixty to seventy miles a day and preached an average of three sermons a day.

When Alexander Maclaren went into his study, he took off his slippers and put on working boots, because he knew that a minister of God is to be a working man.

Because our Lord worked hard, He was weary, and yet He went on ministering. His example calls us to go for it all, to expand our hearts, and by doing so, to become more vulnerable to pain and disappointment.

Overcoming Barriers

> There came a woman of Samaria to draw water. Jesus said to her, "Give Me a drink." For His disciples had gone away into the city to buy food. The Samaritan woman therefore said to Him, "How is it that You, being a Jew, ask me for a drink since I am a Samaritan woman?" (For Jews have no dealings with Samaritans.) (John 4:7-9)

The bitter hatred between the Jews and Samaritans was of long standing. In 721 B.C., the Assyrians swept through the Northern Kingdom of Israel and took the inhabitants to Assyria. During the years of captivity, the Jews intermarried with the Assyrians and the Cuthites.

In 587 B.C., Babylon took captive the people of Judah, the Southern Kingdom, but they did not intermarry in Babylon and when these Jews returned to their homes they were still of unadulterated Jewish blood, unlike the people of the north. As a result, the people of Judah refused to accept their northern kinsmen. Both sides developed an implacable hatred for the other.

The Jewish rabbis said, "Let no man eat the bread of the Cuthites (the Samaritans), for he who eats their bread is as he who eats swine's flesh." A popular prayer in those days went something like this: "And Lord, do not remember the Samaritans in the resurrection."

At the well of Sychar Jesus disregarded this long-standing barrier and spoke to a Samaritan, and another barrier by talking with a woman. Strict rabbis forbade other rabbis to greet a woman in public. Some Pharisees, called "bruised and bleeding Pharisees" covered their eyes when they saw a woman in public and then bumped into walls and houses as they walked about.

Jesus not only spoke to the woman, but He asked to use her drinking utensil—and thereby became defiled. Just how extraordinary His request was, is underlined by Alexander

Maclaren's description of the surroundings:

> When these words were spoken, the then-known civilized world was cleft by great, deep gulfs of separation, like the crevasses in a glacier, by the side of which our racial animosities and class differences are merely superficial cracks on the surface. Language, religion, national animosities, differences of condition, and saddest of all, difference of sex, split the world up into alien fragments. A "stranger" and an "enemy" were expressed in one language, by the same word. The learned and the unlearned, the slave and his master, the barbarian and the Greek, the man and the woman, stood on opposite sides of the gulfs, flinging hostility across. . . . Then the benefits of the Gospel came! Then "the Barbarian, Scythian, bond and free, male and female, Jew and Greek, learned and ignorant," clasped hands and sat down at one table, and felt themselves "all one in Christ Jesus." They were ready to break all bonds (*Expositions of Holy Scripture,* Baker, Vol. 11, pp. 227-228).

When the ancient world saw this, it accused the Christians of sorcery because it could not understand this bridging of barriers. The great glory of the church is that the Gospel crosses barriers.

It is in vogue today to insist that likes win likes. That doctors best evangelize doctors, athletes best evangelize athletes, and ethnics best evangelize their own. I personally do not believe this is the ideal. While there are pragmatic reasons why this approach may work well at times, I believe the ideal is for every Christian to have a heart so filled with love that he is willing to go the extra mile and bridge social barriers.

Jesus calls us to have ministering hearts, to reach out to others in spite of the barriers. This is the mark of the authentic disciple of Christ.

Perhaps you need to take some steps, to cross some barriers. Perhaps you need to rub elbows with people who are not like you, to reach out to them with a ministering heart.

Awareness of Divine Arrangement

This story suggests another quality of the ministering heart. As it goes about its daily business, passing from person to person, it is proceeding from divine appointment to divine appointment. Jesus was aware of the divine arrangement of human acquaintance. "And He had to pass through Samaria" (v. 4). Jesus was aware of and submissive to the sovereign ordering of His life that brought people His way.

Though it was many years ago, I remember well the frustration of traveling 250 miles across the Mojave Desert to take a group of young people on a Christian service project. When we arrived in Parker, Arizona we couldn't find a place to camp. We drove up and down the stretch of river until it was almost dark. Finally, we pulled into a camp and found a place to pitch our tents. We soon discovered that we were camped next to five high school boys who lived twenty miles from our church in California. They were drunk and rude. The situation looked impossible. I wondered why we were forced to spend a week under such difficult circumstances. As the week progressed and the boys ran out of alcohol, they began to warm to the claims of the Gospel. All five eventually trusted Christ, and today three of them are in the ministry. My frustration was really a prelude to God's sovereign appointment.

Stuart Briscoe tells a story about the time he and his wife Jill, were working with Ian Thomas in northern England. One particular day, Stuart had to be away from Capernwray Bible School, where they were teaching, and he left the car for his wife. After he had gone, she realized that he had the car keys in his pocket. She finally was able to borrow a car and was on her way down the road when she saw some girls walking. She stopped to give them a ride and found out that they were from Germany and visiting in England.

As they rode, Jill told the girls about a Christian conference she was going to that day, and persuaded them to come with her. One of the girls, a theological student in Germany, was saved that evening, and told Jill her story.

She had come under the influence of some teaching that had filled her with doubt and confusion. As a result, she had delivered an ultimatum to God—"If You are there, You have to show Yourself to me in some way within the next three months. If You don't, I am going to quit school, forget about theology and religion, and I may quit living, since there is nothing to live for."

With great emotion she looked at Jill and said, "The three months end today" (Stuart Briscoe, *Bound for Joy,* Regal, pp. 20-21).

A ministering heart is aware of the sovereign ordering of life. It is sobering to think that we never talk to a mere mortal. Everyone we meet will live eternally, either as a glorified child of God or as a lost and condemned soul. The ministering heart senses this and treats all encounters as if they come from the hand of God.

To love at all is to be vulnerable. Love anything, and your heart will certainly be wrung and possibly be broken. If you want to make sure of keeping it intact, you must give your heart to no one, not even to an animal. Wrap it carefully round with hobbies and little luxuries; avoid all entanglements; lock it up safe in the casket or coffin of your selfishness. But in that casket—safe, dark, motionless, airless—it will change. It will not be broken; it will become unbreakable, impenetrable, irredeemable. The alternative to tragedy, or at least to the risk of tragedy, is damnation. The only place outside heaven where you can be perfectly safe from all the dangers and perturbations of love is hell (C.S. Lewis, *The Four Loves,* Harcourt, Brace, Jovanovich, p. 169).

If you are wounded and recoiling, wondering if you will ever again allow yourself to be vulnerable, let Jesus strengthen your heart and lead you in His ways.

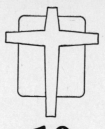

10
Genuine Worship

I wonder if there was ever a time when true spiritual worship was at a lower ebb. To great sections of the church the art of worship has been lost entirely, and in its place has come that strange and foreign thing called the *program*. This word has been borrowed from the stage and applied with sad wisdom to the type of public service which now passes for worship among us (A.W. Tozer, *The Pursuit of God*, Tyndale, p. 9).

Dr. Tozer wrote this in 1948, but his words still apply. An upward focus is sadly absent in many churches. It is easy to be more interested in the mechanics of worship than in the quality, in the place than in our preparation for worship.

Karl Barth wrote, "Christian worship is the most momentous, most urgent, most glorious action that can take place in human life."

We see this in Jesus' conversation with the Samaritan woman. She asked which mountain was the proper place to worship. This is the kind of question people ask today:

"Woman, believe Me, an hour is coming when neither in this mountain, nor in Jerusalem, shall you worship the Father. You worship that which you do not know; we worship that which we know, for salvation is from the Jews. But an hour is coming, and now is, when the true worshipers shall worship the Father in spirit and truth; for such people the Father seeks to be His worshipers. God is Spirit, and those who worship Him must worship in spirit and truth" (John 4:21-24).

The Lord told her that the place of worship was irrelevant and that the Jews worshiped with a superior knowledge. He probably explained that this was because the Samaritans used only the first five books of the Bible and were thus limited in their knowledge. She didn't ask the most important question, "What does God require in worship?" Though she didn't ask it, Jesus answered it for her eternal benefit—and ours. It is to worship in spirit and in truth (v. 24).

Worship in Spirit
Jesus did not say, "Worship in the Spirit" with a capital *S.* He was talking about the human spirit and meant that God is looking for those who will worship Him in the depth of their inner beings. This is authentic worship.

Outward performance may or may not be worship. We can sing and pray aloud and yet not worship. We can give and not be giving ourselves to God in worship.

We can kneel in the most beautiful cathedrals, listen to the most concise and biblical liturgy, and luxuriate in the strains of evensong, but not be worshiping. We can do none of these and yet have entered into the deepest worship. Outward circumstances do not determine the authenticity of worship.

This is not to say that externals are not helpful, for they are. Yet generally, I think C.S. Lewis was right when he said that the best church service is the one we notice the least.

As long as you notice, and have to count the steps, you are not yet dancing but only learning to dance. A good shoe is a shoe you don't notice. Good reading becomes possible when you need not consciously think about eyes, or light, or print, or spelling. The perfect church service would be the one we were almost unaware of; our attention would have been on God (*Letters to Malcolm Chiefly on Prayer*, Harcourt, Brace, and World, p. 4).

Some of the most precious worship recorded in Scripture took place in the least conducive environment. It was midnight and Paul and Silas had just been stripped of their clothes, beaten with rods, and fastened in stocks in the depths of the Philippian jail. In their misery, backs bleeding, and confined so that they could neither sit straight nor sleep nor move without pain, Silas and Paul began praying and singing hymns of praise to God (Acts 16:25). Despite their circumstances, worship bubbled forth. True worship can happen anywhere.

Since the human spirits of believers have been touched by the Holy Spirit, we have expanded capacity and a deeper hunger for worship. New believers often can't get enough worship. However, if this hunger is not fed, it may starve.

A major flaw of today's Christianity is insufficient provision for worship. As a consequence, people sense an incompleteness. Children raised in this type of environment may later leave their orthodoxy for empty forms that massage their need to worship. It is important that we provide the experiences of worship that believers need.

Worship in Truth

Worshiping in truth is worshiping in accord with what God has revealed about Himself. The converse is also true. True worship does *not* take place when we do not worship in accord with what God has revealed about Himself. What we believe about God is of the greatest importance. Creedal statements are good; however, subscribing to such a statement does not necessarily indicate what we really believe, because it is possible to mouth the words and not mean what they say. Or we can be indifferent.

What comes to your mind when you think about God? What we think of Him affects our worship and our living. Most failures in worship and errors in doctrine or practice can be traced to wrong thoughts about God. Wrong thoughts about God were the source of Cain's failure to worship as he should have. He brought a sacrifice to fit his personal concept of God. He thought, "Why in the world would God want an unattractive and bloody sacrifice, when I could bring Him something beautiful from my field?"

At the beginning of recorded history, we see a man implicitly distorting what had been revealed about God. He followed his own imagining rather than what he had been told.

So necessary to the church is a correct concept of God that when it is blurred, worship suffers and moral standards decline. I believe one reason for the divorce problem today is a lack of teaching about the person of God. When we recognize who God is and what He requires, and when we subscribe to this knowledge, we take seriously His ordained relationships in our lives.

Wrong thinking about God is really idolatry, because an idolatrous heart assumes that God is other than He is. We must not think that we, in our sophisticated and civilized times, are free of idolatry.

The typical twentieth-century view of God is decadent. Some see Him only as a cosmic force. Certain theologians call Him the ground of being. People who conceive of God in these ways will worship Him with icy reverence. At the other extreme are those who think of God as a pal. Everything in their religious lives is essentially centered on themselves and what God can do for them. He has become a cosmic slot machine. Instead of inserting quarters, people put in Scripture verses to get what they want from Him. This is the most popular idea today—the God who gives to me. Awe and reverence are missing.

God Seeks Genuine Worship

The central fact in a time of worship is not that we are seeking God, but that He is seeking us. This is a totally Christian idea. Most Jews of Jesus' day never thought of God this way. The wonderful thing about worship is that the expectancy within us is only a shadow of God's expectancy at receiving us. "He will rejoice over you with shouts of joy" (Zeph. 3:17).

To worship rightly we first need to be people of the Word, because the clearest revelation of God is in His Word. When Jesus prayed His high priestly prayer, He said, "Sanctify them in the truth; Thy Word is truth" (John 17:17)—especially truth about God. When we are filled with the Word, the attributes of God and the metaphors which describe Him become the praise of our hearts, for worship can take place only as we return to God what He has revealed about Himself.

We also need to realize that worship is a challenging activity which involves mental interaction with the truth about God. In worship, we develop the ability to hold contrasting truths about God in "devotional tension." That is, we see Him as the mighty, eternal, transcendant Creator who holds the universe together, and at the same time as the One who said, "O Jerusalem. . . . How often I wanted to gather your children together, the way a hen gathers her chicks under her wings" (Matt. 23:37). To worship only one or two attributes of God is not worshiping Him in truth. Worship must include the total revelation of God. Then idolatrous hearts are purged, moral standards elevated, and God is pleased.

The Samaritan woman who first heard these great truths about worship did not have our privileges. Yet she worshiped. The Samaritans had a belief that a prophet like Moses would be raised up to explain the Law. They called Him the *Taheb*. When the woman speculated about who Jesus might be, she said, "I know that Messiah is coming (He who is called Christ); when that One comes, He will declare all things to us" (John 4:25).

Jesus' reply to her was, "I who speak to you am He" (v. 26).

The first requisite to worshiping in spirit and in truth is to meet the Messiah, as the Samaritan woman did, and to receive Him in the truth of who He is.

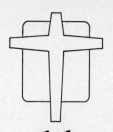

11
Thinking Rightly about God's love

In Jesus' famous exchange with the Samaritan woman at the well, He told her the Father seeks worshipers:

"But an hour is coming, and now is, when the true worshipers shall worship the Father in spirit and truth; for such people the Father seeks to be His worshipers. God is Spirit; and those who worship Him must worship in spirit and truth" (John 4:23-24).

We see a divine poignancy in this, because the fact that God has to *seek* worshipers tells us that few people really worship Him in spirit and in truth. Having the truth is not enough. History reveals that many people who know the truth of God do not worship Him in spirit because the truth never penetrates their lives.

The key to the worship God seeks is in experiencing the reality of the love of God which has been poured out within our hearts through the Holy Spirit (Rom. 5:5). God is seeking those who will love Him with all of their hearts. Yet it is at this very point—the love of God—where people most often think wrongly about God. When we fail to understand the love of God, we fail to understand His other attributes, because His love controls all of these.

Wrong Views of God's Love

Several years ago a pastor performed a wedding which he was sure would produce a winning marriage. He had known the young couple for years. Both came from strong Christian families, both had given their lives to Christ, both were musical, both were athletic—and both were committed to the mission field.

The couple was given a beautiful wedding and embarked on a life of great potential. They energetically attacked their work. They were unusually effective in their local church, even though their focus was on the foreign mission field. When they departed, almost the entire church turned out to wish them bon voyage.

The pastor was immensely shocked when two years later the young husband suddenly appeared in his office unannounced and said through tears, "My wife is divorcing me. She does not want to be my wife. She doesn't want to be a missionary's wife. She will give no other reason."

Nothing could dissuade her. They were divorced and he is out of the ministry. You may think there was more to it than this, and there was, but not much more. She simply didn't love her husband and was unhappy. She wouldn't listen to anyone—not parents, friends, pastors, or counselors. The rationale with which she fortified herself as she acted to dissolve the marriage was, "I am not happy. God loves me and wants me to be happy; therefore, this marriage is not God's will. A loving God would not want me to spend my life with a man I do not love, because God wants me to be happy."

Her understanding of God's love affected the way she lived. The truth, "God is love" filtered through her mind as "God exists to make me happy, according to my definition of happiness." This is functional heresy and idolatry.

Wrong Concepts of God

A wrong concept of God permeates modern parenting. Never have parents been so convinced of their responsibility to make their children happy. Their unfortunate thinking goes something like this: "A loving parent will attentively do everything he can to make a child happy—according to the child's definition."

This idea is so prevalent that the *Los Angeles Times* carried an article explaining why many young couples were not having children. One of the major reasons was that they did not want to take on the obligation of making someone else happy. The article theorized that the problem stems from the fact that many of today's young adults were brought up by parents who made them believe that their children's happiness was the most important. Whatever the reason, many parents and children today are subjects of a vicious belief: "You have not made me happy as I desire; therefore, you do not love me."

Such thinking doesn't stop with parents and children or husbands and wives, but carries into other relationships, including a real or imagined relationship with God. Some people picture Him nervously biting His fingernails as He tries to find creative ways to keep His children happy, according to their definitions of happiness.

A person in this frame of mind projects bizarre interpretations on Scripture. For instance, the truth of John 3:16, that "God so loved the world, that He gave His only begotten Son," is appropriated to suggest that the sacrificial agonies Christ endured on the cross illustrate what He goes through to procure our day-to-day happiness—that God will do or allow anything to make us happy.

Such thinking extends to personal desires: "I cannot be happy until I am financially secure; therefore, it is God's will that I be successful financially because He loves me." There are preachers today who proclaim that if we follow Christ, we will be well-off. Another desire is for good health: "I cannot be happy when I am sick; therefore, it is not God's will that I be ill because God loves me." The final and most absurd desire is a form of self-idolatry which says: "God loves me so much that His happiness is bound up with mine. When I am happy, God is happy. Whatever makes me happy makes God happy."

This perverted thinking about God's love goes hand in hand with the narcissism of our times. Narcissus, you'll remember, was a Greek god who one day walked beside a pond, looked down, and saw his reflection. He fell so in love with his reflection that he never got over it. He couldn't love anyone besides himself.

Commenting on the "meism" of our day, Alexander Solzhenitsyn said:

> We have become hopelessly enmeshed in a slavish worship of all that is pleasant, all that is comfortable, all that is material. We worship things. We worship products.

He could well have added that we worship happiness. When "God is love" is translated, "God is Mr. Goodbar," we have reached the very nadir of religious idolatry. We are no better than the pagan who worships a god of his own making, one he thinks will supply him with a happiness of his own imagining.

How do you think about God's love?

The Truth About God's Love

God's love never conflicts with His holiness and righteousness. His love is regulated by principle, not by sentiment. God operates from a complete perspective and surrounds us not only with His love but also with His truth, virtue, goodness, and holiness. Because He is holy, He seeks holiness for those He loves. He never condones actions which are not consonant with His holiness. He does not fall into the weak-minded errors of an indulgent parent. He is not deceived by His children's foolish plans for temporary happiness.

God cares far more for our happiness than we do, and does not want us to settle for lower levels of something we call happiness. God wants the highest for us, and He is not in a hurry. We usually are.

God's formula for happiness is found in the Sermon on the Mount:

How happy are the humble-minded, for the kingdom of heaven is theirs! How happy are those who know what sorrow means, for they will be given courage and comfort! Happy are those who claim nothing, for the whole earth will belong to them! Happy are those who are hungry and thirsty for goodness, for they shall be fully satisfied! Happy are the merciful, for they will have mercy shown to them! Happy are the utterly sincere, for they will see God! Happy are those who make peace, for they will be known as sons of God! Happy are those who have suffered persecution for the cause of goodness, for the kingdom of heaven is theirs! And what happiness will be yours when people blame you and ill-treat you and say all kinds of slanderous things against you for My sake! (Matt. 5:3-11, PH)

Happiness is having God's character in our lives. The possibility for this kind of happiness springs from the fact that God's *agape* love has two aspects—intelligence and will. In His love, God sees with greater intelligence, from a wider perspective, what real happiness is. With this real happiness in mind, God wills that we be happy.

Along with His *agape* love is the fact that God is always good. From the first chapter of Genesis to the end of the Book of Revelation, we see testimony that God is good. He is always good, for He never changes.

These thoughts naturally lead to the truth that His goodness has caused Him to identify Himself with our welfare. He has bound up His happiness with ours in the sense of happiness by *His definition.*

J.I. Packer in his book *Knowing God* affirms this:

God was happy without man before man was made; He would have continued happy had He simply destroyed man after man had sinned; but as it is He has set His love upon particular sinners, and this means that, by His own free voluntary choice, He will not know perfect and unmixed happiness again till He has brought every one of them to heaven. He has in effect resolved that henceforth for all eternity His happiness shall be conditional upon ours. Thus God saves, not only for His glory, but also for His gladness. This goes far to explain why it is that there is joy (God's own joy) in the presence of the angels when a sinner repents (Luke 15:10), and why there will be "exceeding joy" when God sets us faultless at the last day in His own holy presence (Jude 24). The thought passes understanding and almost beggars belief, but there is no doubt that, according to Scripture, such is the love of God (InterVarsity, p. 113).

When God decided to love us, He elected not to know perfect and unmixed happiness until we are perfected. This is the nature of love, because love expands the heart and attaches its happiness to the object that it loves. For some reason known only in God's wisdom, He has attached His happiness to ours. It is a logical implication of His incarnation and of His death. This is thinking rightly about God.

Paul wrote that the love of Christ surpasses knowledge (Eph. 3:19). Literally translated, this means *supersurpasses* knowledge.

Years ago, Leslie Weatherhead, a famous English preacher, was on a Mediterranean cruise when he witnessed an unexpected midnight eruption of the island volcano Stromboli. Weatherhead described how the whole sky was aglow with a marvelous display which he and the other passengers watched for hours till it faded off beyond the horizon. Being a preacher, Weatherhead reflected on the meaning of what had occurred and concluded that what they had seen was a brief revelation of the fires which had been burning in the mountain's heart since the foundation of the world. Then as he thought of God, he wrote these words:

> I sometimes think about the Cross,
> And shut my eyes, and try to see
> The cruel nails and crown of thorns,
> And Jesus, crucified for me.
> But, even could I see Him die,
> I could but see a little part
> Of that great love, which, like a fire,
> Is always burning in His heart.
> (*His Life and Ours,* Abingdon Cokesbury, p. 275)

The Measure of Love

The measure of someone's love is how much he is willing to give. The measure of our Lord's love is the Cross, where we have seen something of the infinite fire of His love.

Because God is self-existent, His love had no beginning; because He is eternal, His love can have no end; because He is infinite, it has no limit; because He is holy, it is the quintessence of all spotless purity; because He is immense, His love is an incomprehensibly vast, bottomless, shoreless sea (A.W. Tozer, *The Knowledge of the Holy,* Harper and Row, p. 105).

All His attributes are brought to focus on us in the infinity of His love. God does not want His children to settle for a shabby imitation of happiness. He pursues us and urges us on to real happiness.

If we can learn to hold the truth about God's love in the devotional tension of living, we will be blessed. We will be those who worship Him in spirit and in truth.

12
Believing Is Seeing

Money can buy a king-sized bed, but it can't buy sleep. Money can buy a great house, but it can't buy a home. Money can buy a companion, but it can't buy lasting friendship. Money can buy books, but it can't buy brains. Money can buy a church building, but it can't buy heaven.

Money can buy medical care, but it can't buy health. The nobleman of Capernaum knew this, because he had sought help for his sick child and yet the child was dying. When he heard that Jesus had come back to Cana, where He had turned water into wine at a wedding, the nobleman decided to ask this Rabbi to heal his son.

In our text, the nobleman is called a royal official. The word in Greek is *basilikos,* which can be translated nobleman, king's man, or petty king. This *basilikos* was evidently an official in Herod's court and a man of great influence. He was also a man of great wealth, as Herod's men were apt to be. By anyone's standards, he was a man who had everything he could possibly want, except for one thing—his son was very ill. The child had contracted a fever, and the father had watched as the boy's life slowly drained away. The color faded from the young face, the light in the eyes dimmed so that at times he stared but did not see. Eventually the boy lapsed into intermittent coma, indicating that death was near.

Nothing can shatter a parent more than a child's illness. Hearing the doctor's diagnosis, as my wife did, that our child had spinal meningitis—and then watching the doctor withdraw that huge hypodermic needle from our child's spine—turns life celluloid gray. We wandered from lab to clinic to doctor, feeling like useless characters in a long-forgotten story, and thinking, "This cannot be happening!"

I understand how the nobleman felt. He found himself enshrouded in a grim darkness, because the light of his life was about to expire. Though children carry a sense of immortality, the fact is that they do die. All I have to do is look back in my own ministry at the funerals for children. We can visit a graveyard and look at the many small graves and read the tombstones to see that those buried there lived only a few years. In the history of mankind, the first grave was dug for Abel, a young man.

Regardless of our station in life, trouble, sorrow, and death come to all. Death was knocking at the door of the *basilikos*, as it does in homes today.

Word of Jesus' arrival in Cana must have sparked a glimmer of hope, for the nobleman quickly set off for Cana, the pounding of his horse's hooves a reflection of his heartbeat.

I like this nobleman. He came to Jesus himself. He did not send a servant. He did not send his wife. This nobleman was involved with his family. He cared for his children and he personally took on this important errand.

A Cry for Help

When he heard that Jesus had come out of Judea into Galilee, he went to Him, and was requesting Him to come down and heal his son; for he was at the point of death (John 4:47).

We can visualize the encounter between the nobleman and Jesus, the carpenter. A man of wealth and power meeting a man with neither wealth nor power. The word *requesting* means that the nobleman began to beg and kept it up. He was indifferent to the noise around him, unaware of the crowd, as he followed Jesus saying, "Lord, Sir, heal my son!"

Our Lord's reply to him is startling. "Unless you people see signs and wonders, you simply will not believe" (v. 48). That was Jesus' answer to a man's pathetic cry for his child? On the surface, it seems a detached, coldly unsympathetic response. Actually, Jesus' reply was full of grace. His words were mercifully surgical. When He said "you," it was plural. "Unless you *people* see signs and wonders, you simply will not believe." He was referring not only to the nobleman, but also to the Galileans whose tendency the nobleman represented. Jesus' words were going to lift the father to new levels of faith, and also anyone else who would listen and respond.

In C.S. Lewis' autobiography, *Surprised by Joy,* he relates how he was brought kicking and struggling into the kingdom of God, eyes darting every which way for a path of escape. Then he reflects, "The hardness of God is kinder than the softness of men, and His compulsion is our liberation" (Harcourt, Brace, and World, p. 229).

With unerring accuracy our Lord put His finger on the weakness of the people's faith. They focused on signs and wonders. They were following Jesus as if He were a religious sideshow— "Hurry, hurry, don't miss the latest miracle! Get your bagels here. Crowd in close, folks, so you can see the new miracle." People were focusing on signs to the extent that they were missing Jesus' true identity. The nobleman seems also to have been confused, because of his repeated emphasis on Jesus coming down to Capernaum to heal his son. He wanted Jesus to do His "good magic" to heal his son.

We ought not miss the obvious application to our own day. Some Christians constantly seek for signs and wonders to confirm their faith. Such people may be missing the intention of the signs, Christ Himself. If we focus on sensationalism, miracles, and signs, it may be that we are not looking to Christ who alone is sufficient.

At the same time, it is important to know that Jesus was not deprecating miracles. He was about to perform one—one that would lead the father on to faith in Him. The thrust of what Jesus was saying is, "Oh, that you might think less about the wonders and more about Me!"

Because it is easier for us today to focus on the visible and the immediate, we too need to follow along with the *basilikos* in his lesson of faith.

Test of Faith

The nobleman responded to Jesus, "Sir, come down before my child dies" (v. 49). He did not deny Jesus' charge nor did he assert his position. He seemed to express a spirit similar to the Syrophoenician woman, who said, "Even the dogs feed on the crumbs which fall from their master's table" (Matt. 15:27). His attitude was like that of John Bunyan:

> I was driven to such straits that I must of necessity go to Jesus; and if He had met me with a drawn sword in His hand, I would sooner have thrown myself upon the edge of His sword than have gone away from Him; for I knew Him to be my last hope (C.H. Spurgeon, *Metropolitan Tabernacle Pulpit,* Pilgrim, Vol. 31, p. 571).

Jesus was this man's last hope and he was not leaving Him. He did not try to pull rank and say, "Now, listen here, Carpenter, this young boy has royal blood." Rather, he took hold of as much as he could comprehend of Jesus' character and pathetically cried, "Sir, come down before my child dies" (John 4:49). It was a cry for mercy.

Jesus' reply contained a partial granting and a partial denial. "Go your way; your son lives" (v. 50). He granted the healing but refused to go down to Capernaum. He gave him no sign. He gave only His word. In the awesome silence of that moment, as Jesus said, "Go your way; your son lives," what must have been going on in the nobleman's mind? We know that he took the step of faith, for we read, "The man believed the word that Jesus spoke to him and he started off" (v. 50). He didn't argue, plead, insist on "just a little sign." He simply remembered the testimony of his servants concerning the wedding miracle—and what He had heard from the people of Cana—and he saw Jesus before him. He believed.

What happened to him is quite the reverse of the common "Seeing is believing" attitude in our world. For the nobleman, "believing was seeing." His belief was such that even with eighteen miles between them, he saw his boy in good health.

Seeing the Unseen
The testimony of Scripture is unified about the revelation of faith and sight. Later, Jesus spoke of Abraham's faith "Your Father Abraham rejoiced to see My day" (8:56), meaning that because of faith in what God said, Abraham saw the day of the Gospel. He saw the unseen.

In the Book of Hebrews we read of others who saw with the eyes of faith:

All these died in faith, without receiving the promises, but having seen them and having welcomed them from a distance, and having confessed that they were strangers and exiles on earth (11:13).

By faith they saw the promises fulfilled. Of Moses we read, "By faith he left Egypt, not fearing the wrath of the king; for he endured, as seeing Him who is unseen" (Heb. 11:27). Moses' faith enabled him to see the unseen.

What is this faith? It is defined in Hebrews 11:1:

Now faith is the assurance of things hoped for, the conviction of things not seen.

Now faith is the substance of things hoped for, the evidence of things not seen (KJV).

And what is faith? Faith gives substance to our hopes, and makes us certain of realities we do not see (NEB).

Now faith means putting our full confidence in the things we hope for; it means being certain of things we cannot see (PH).

What is faith? It is the confident assurance that something we want is going to happen. It is the certainty that what we hope for is waiting for us, even though we cannot see it up ahead (TLB).

Faith sees the unseen. Believing is seeing. It is faith that gives living color to God's words. "We know that God causes all things to work together for good to those who love God, to those who are called according to His purpose" (Rom. 8:28). Apart from the illumination of faith, this is just an ancient maxim. Seen through the lens of faith, it flames alive. We see the unseen—our trouble resulting in good.

On the basis of Jesus' words, the nobleman saw his child healthy and well, the color back in his cheeks. The father believed with such conviction that "he started off."

And as he was now going down, his slaves met him, saying that his son was living. So he inquired of them the hour when he began to get better. They said therefore to him, "Yesterday at the seventh hour the fever left him." So the father knew that it was at that hour in which Jesus said to him, "Your son lives" (John 4:51-53).

The Leisure of Faith

Did you notice that word *yesterday?* I find this amazing. If he had left Cana at the seventh hour, or one in the afternoon, and had hurried back to Capernaum, he would have arrived home by five that same afternoon, but he didn't get home until the next day. He so thoroughly believed that he stayed in Cana, perhaps to take care of some business or to talk with the disciples. Maybe he spent some time with Jesus. What faith!

When he met his servants on the road and they informed him of the recovery, he asked what time it happened. When they replied it was at one in the afternoon, he checked his sundial and said, "Just what I thought." The difference between his urgent trip to Cana and his leisurely one home was faith.

We all have problems and pressures. Some deal with them in a rushed, frenetic way. Others have learned to take them in the leisure of faith that believes God is as good as His word.

The nobleman's faith was crowned. He had learned who Christ is and had trusted in Him. When he returned home, his whole household believed also.

Two conditions bring forth faith. The first is to *hear* God's Word. "Faith comes from hearing, and hearing by the Word of Christ" (Rom. 10:17). We need to immerse ourselves in the Word of God so that our faith can grow. In Colossians we read, "Let the Word of Christ richly dwell within you" (3:16).

The second condition to the growth of faith is to *exercise* it. Maclaren of Manchester said it well:

> The way to increase faith is to exercise faith. And the true parent of perfect faith is the experience of the blessings that come from the crudest, rudest, narrowest, blindest, feeblest faith that a man can exercise. Trust Him as you can, do not be afraid of inadequate conceptions, or of a feeble grasp. Trust Him as you can, and He will give you so much more than you expected that you will trust Him more (*Expositions of Holy Scripture,* Baker, Vol. 10, pp. 234-35).

We all have opportunities to grow in faith because we all have difficulties. If in our troubles, we turn to the Word of God, it will speak to us. If we believe on the Word, and act on it, we will grow in faith.

"The hardness of God is kinder than the softness of men, and His compulsion is our liberation." If you have a sense of closing darkness, a feeling of futility in your life, you may be on the verge of great blessing—if you turn to God. You have heard that there is One who can meet your need. Fly to His feet. Tell Him your need. Hear His words. Then obey Him. You will find life—full growing life through faith.

13
Allowing Christ to Work in Us

It is not difficult to gather people to the site where a miracle is said to have happened. The shrines and holy places of the world are testimonies to this. When we lived in California, a woman there claimed to have had revelations from St. Joseph. Soon after she shared her experience large crowds began to gather around her house. In time, people from around the world made pilgrimages to see her. Bumper stickers announced, "St. Joseph has appeared." Just outside her town, 400 acres were purchased to build St. Joseph's Hill of Hope. St. Joseph is reported to have appeared there and revealed where water was to be found on the property. Today armed guards stand at the entrance to the Hill of Hope.

Our experience with the shrines of the world helps us to understand the story in John 5:1-18. The Pool of Bethesda was a sort of shrine. The pool periodically rippled because of a subterranean spring. Long before, a sick person had been in the pool when it rippled and he had concluded that he was healed by the water. News of the "miracle" spread over the city and surrounding countryside and a legend was born: At certain seasons an angel of the Lord went down into the pool, and stirred up the water. The first person to go into the pool after the stirring would be healed (v. 4). As a result, hundreds of people from the countryside came to the Pool of Bethesda to be healed. Five porticoes were built so that the sick could be shaded from the sun as they waited for the stirring of the waters. The construction was probably financed by those who were thrilled at what was said to be happening—people similar to the ones who financed the Hill of Hope in California.

The crowd around the pool must have been a pathetic sight. We read that there were not just a few sick people, but a multitude, probably hundreds. Some were so feverish they had to stay in the shade because the heat of the sun was unbearable. The blind must have huddled close to the edge of the pool, hoping someone would lead them in when the waters quivered. The withered and the lame could not make it to the pool by themselves and had to be carried in. It was a distressing sight except that on this day, Jesus was there.

Our Lord was alone. Without His disciples, He could travel unnoticed. His gaze rested on one of the worst cases, a man who had been confined to bed for thirty-eight years. He had never been able to reach the pool in time.

Questions We Don't Ask

Jesus asked the man, "Do you wish to get well?" (v. 6) It seems a ridiculous question to ask a man who has been ill for thirty-eight years. In our dealings with people, we just don't ask some questions. For instance, when I am out in a boat fishing for a spot where the fish are biting, I never ask other fishermen if they are catching anything. If they are, they will say, "We've had a few bites." If they aren't, they will resent the question.

When you see a car stalled at the side of the road and a man leaning under the hood, you don't say, "Is there something wrong with your car?" You are liable to hear, "No, I'm under here hugging my carburetor." Or worse.

In all my years of hospital visitation, I have never stood

beside a sickbed and inquired, "Do you wish to get well?" So I am sure I would not have asked the paralytic that question. At first it might seem a cruel question, and yet I believe it is a question that He asks of all of us, addressing, reaching into the quality of our devotional experience with the Lord. "Do you want to be well?"

No Change

Do we really want Christ to work in our lives? The gracious work of Christ in our lives is hampered because of our answer to this question. Our hearts are warmed when we first hear the promises of God. We hear them again, and our hearts are still warmed, but nothing happens. The cycle continues. We hear and think we respond, but no change results. Though we think and say that we want to be healed, in our hearts we really do not.

For the paralytic man, Jesus' query had economic significance. J.A. Findley tells us that in the Middle East, in Jesus' time and now, a man who was healed would lose a good living from begging. As the paralytic lay by the Pool of Bethesda, he was surrounded by misery and sorrow, and yet he was cared for. If he looked out beyond the shaded porticoes, he could see men and women working in the sun. If he was to be healed, his life would take on larger responsibilities. Jesus' question was relevant: "Do you really want to be healed?"

Jesus asks this question of those who seek His salvation. The French philosopher Pascal put it this way: "Men often mistake the imagination for the heart; they believe they are converted as soon as they think of being converted." Why did Pascal believe this? Because what Christ offers looks so wonderful from a distance, yet when we examine it closely it may appear less desirable. We may begin to understand that Christ expects certain requirements of us.

I have seen people attend church over a period of time, even sitting on the front row. They are respectful and interested in what they are hearing. Though they are not converted, they are listening to the Gospel. Then a time comes when they realize they do not want to be converted. They leave, not to another faith or church. They just leave.

This question also comes to Christians, for often we do not know what is in our hearts. The more we come to know ourselves, the more we find that needs to be healed: bitterness, unresolved conflicts, old hurts. When we first experienced the cause of these wounds, we were aware of them, but we didn't deal with them. We cauterized them, layered them over, and they still affect our lives. They take their toll. We don't experience God's power. We don't feel authentic. We don't have inner peace. The unresolved sin or hurt in our lives is submerged into our unconscious.

"Do you really want to be healed?" Do you want the bitterness and conflict resolved? If you do, God will reveal to you what must be cleansed. As we live with His continued healing, we are blessed with the release and joy that comes from having the slate clean with God.

Realizing We Are Helpless

The paralytic answered Jesus, "Sir, I have no man to put me into the pool when the water is stirred up, but while I am coming, another steps down before me" (v. 7). This man had no problem realizing that he couldn't manage the healing by himself. All those years of not being able to get to the water in time had convinced him. For those plagued with spiritual or emotional paralysis, admitting their inability is not so simple. They often imagine that they can do something themselves.

It seems that the paralytic truly did want to be healed, but he needed faith before he could be made whole. While his faith is certainly not explicit in our text, I believe it is implicit. When he realized he couldn't heal himself, he looked in obedience to Christ, who instructed him, " 'Arise, take up your pallet, and walk.' And immediately the man became well, and took up his pallet and began to walk" (vv. 8-9).

As he began to stand, he found that his legs straightened and he had the power to walk. His experience was rather like that of the people in Moses' day who had been bitten by fiery serpents. At the point of death, they dragged themselves out to look up to the serpent impaled on the pole, and experienced healing (Num. 21:6-9). Christ demands this of us too. We must want to be healed, recognize we cannot do it by ourselves, and look to Him in faith.

Later that Sabbath Day, Jesus encountered the man He had healed in the temple, and said to him, "Behold, you have become well; do not sin anymore, so that nothing worse may befall you" (v. 14).

These words might indicate that Jesus was not confident the man would follow through with the new realities he had experienced. One commentator suggests that the man was unpleasant, the type that no one really would want to help anyway. He does sound weak, yet his weakness and insignificance is a comfort to us. When I honestly look at myself, I have to ask, "Why did Jesus save me?"

After we have known Christ for a while and have come to see our inconsistencies and ungratefulness, we really have to wonder why He didn't drop us along the way.

William Beveridge expressed it for us:

> I cannot pray, except I sin;
> I cannot preach, but I sin;
> I cannot administer, nor receive the holy sacrament,
>   but I sin.
> My very repentence needs to be repented of;
> And the tears I shed need washing in the blood of Christ.
> (James Boice, *The Gospel of John*, Zondervan,
>   Vol. 2, p. 25)

Christ's Reward

The paralytic was an insignificant man who didn't even express gratitude. We who have been saved still are sinners, and yet, one day we will be glorious and radiant.

> Christ also loved the church and gave Himself up for her; that He might sanctify her, having cleansed her by the washing of water with the Word, that He might present to Himself the church in all her glory, having no spot or wrinkle or any such thing; but that she should be holy and blameless (Eph. 5:25-27).

When Christ performed the miracle on the Sabbath, and commanded the man to carry his bed, He widened the breach between Himself and the Pharisees and hastened His own death on the cross. He thought the paralytic was worth the price. He thinks we are worth it too. Though we may not look like it now, someday we are going to be the bride of Christ. He is preparing us for that day.

He wants to release us from whatever is crippling us, whatever is holding us back from being the persons God wants us to become.

Do we *want* to get well?

14
Christ's Identity with the Father

When the Jewish people of Jesus' day thought of God, they saw Him in the imagery of the Old Testament prophets. One of the most vivid pictures of the heavenly hosts and of God Himself is found in the first chapter of Ezekiel. The Prophet Ezekiel saw a cloud approaching him and in it was flashing fire surrounded by an even brighter light. At the center was what appeared to be molten metal, but as the cloud came closer, Ezekiel saw that rather than molten metal there were four human images, each with four faces and four wings. The faces of each image were toward the north, east, south, and west, so that the images never needed to turn.

Besides the images, Ezekiel saw great amber wheels rising into the heavens. Within the wheels were inner wheels, set crosswise so that they had the same freedom of movement as the human images. The rims of the wheels were full of eyes and wherever the living images moved, the wheels went.

Above all of this was a crystal expanse and beyond that a sapphire throne on which sat a human form, surrounded by a glowing rainbow. We know that this figure was Christ, for the revelation given to the Apostle John contains a parallel vision of a figure on a throne who "was like a jasper stone and a sardius in appearance; and there was a rainbow around the throne, like an emerald in appearance" (Rev. 4:3).

The living beings of Ezekiel's vision are a picture of God moving in the accomplishment of His will. The rotating eyes in the wheels represent His omniscence; the luminous expanse speaks of His ineffable glory.

Ezekiel's vision is one of the great foundational Scriptures revealing God and His character. With this background, it is no wonder that when a Hebrew came to the name of God in the Torah, he did not read it, but used Jehovah, the name that is a combination of God's other names. Reverence for the divine name was so great that when the scribes came to the word they would wash their hands before writing it. Nothing could interrupt their writing of the name. Even if a king addressed them while they wrote the sacred name, they would not respond.

It was to people with this understanding of God that Jesus set forth His claims to be One with the Father. We saw the anger of the people because Jesus healed on the Sabbath, and heard His reply, "My Father is working until now and I Myself am working" (John 5:17). Such an answer was intolerable to the Jews and worthy of death, because He called God His Father and made Himself equal to God (v. 18). In the face of their wrath, Jesus did not back down, but continued to claim His identity with the Father in three ways—in action with God, in power to give life, and in authority to judge.

Christ Acts With God

Jesus therefore answered and was saying to them, "Truly, truly, I say to you, the Son can do nothing of Himself, unless it is something He sees the Father doing; for whatever the Father does, these things the Son also does in like manner. For the Father loves the Son, and shows Him all things that He Himself is doing; and greater works than these will He show Him, that you may marvel" (vv. 19-20).

Not only was Jesus claiming identity of action with God the Father; He was also claiming equality with God. God the Father and God the Son do the same works with the same motivation and in the same manner. In our own day, as well as in Jesus' time, people reject the oneness of Jesus with the Father. Television personality Phil Donahue wrote in his autobiography:

> If God the Father is so all-loving, why didn't He come down and go to Calvary? Then Jesus could have said, "This is My Father in whom I am well-pleased." How could an all-knowing, all-loving God allow His Son to be murdered on a cross in order that He might redeem my sins? (*Donahue,* Simon and Schuster, p. 94)

Mr. Donahue's indictment of God's love shows a lack of understanding. Jesus' claims of equality with the Father meant that the Father was a sharer in Jesus' sacrifice and pain, as well as in His love: "The Son can do nothing of Himself, unless it is something He sees the Father doing" (v. 19).

In Jesus' claim to equality with the Father, we see two hearts beating as one. "For the Father loves the Son, and shows Him all things that He Himself is doing" (v. 20).

Christ's hearers who were seeing God in the Old Testament imagery heard Jesus say that He was in those pictures with Jehovah. If we want to see what the Father does, all we need to do is look at Christ who is the likeness of the Father. He is the answer to Donahue's question, as He was to the questions of those who heard Him in Jerusalem.

Because of Jesus' equality with the Father, He is Lord of lords, King of kings. He is supreme. This reality demands a daily response from all who believe so that we affirm Him truly to be Lord in our lives.

Christ Is Lifegiver

"For just as the Father raises the dead and gives them life, even so the Son also gives life to whom He wishes" (v. 21).

"Truly, truly, I say to you, he who hears My Word, and believes Him who sent Me, has eternal life, and does not come into judgment, but has passed out of death into life. Truly, truly, I say to you, an hour is coming and now is, when the dead shall hear the voice of the Son of God; and those who hear shall live. For just as the Father has life in Himself, even so He gave to the Son also to have life in Himself" (vv. 24-26).

Not only did Christ claim equality with God, but He claimed the ability to give life to the spiritually dead.

I remember my own experience of crossing the line from death to life, as a young teenager. I had been raised in the church, and though I was spiritually unregenerated, I was fascinated with the church. It may have been the beauty of the building with its stained glass windows. I recall looking at those windows and being drawn by the mystery of life they suggested. Another attraction to the church was my Bible, a small red-letter edition which I treated with reverence. I found ecclesiastical jargon inviting; I was intrigued by spiritual things. Yet, I knew I was on the outside. I wanted to be inside, wherever inside was.

That summer I went to church camp, and for the first time heard clearly what it meant to be a Christian. In a highly emotional experience, I asked Christ into my life. From the tears I wept, you would think I had committed every sin. In one sense I had. My theology was good, for I knew I was a sinner.

That night I was marvelously born again. As I lay in my sleeping bag, using a flashlight to see, I marked verses in my little Bible which had suddenly come alive for me. For the first time, I felt free of my sin and I had a purpose in life; that night I heard the call to become a minister.

What happened to me is what Christ meant when He said, "Truly, truly, I say to you, an hour is coming and now is, when the dead shall hear the voice of the Son of God; and those who hear shall live" (v. 25).

Thirty years ago, I entered a new realm; I gained eternal life. Not only did I receive this life in a quantitative sense, but I received eternal life qualitatively. My associations changed. My view of work, my relationships to other people, including my family—all entered the process of being changed by what had happened in my life.

We Can Know

Years ago during a sermon, the great preacher G. Campbell Morgan made this statement: "By no means can every Christian remember the time when he was born again." After the service, someone challenged his statement. Morgan turned to the man and asked, "Are you alive?"

The man replied, "Why, of course I am!"

Morgan asked, "Do you remember when you were born?"

The man answered, "Well, I am living."

Morgan replied, "Exactly. Some Christians may not remember the moment of their new birth, but they are spiritually alive and know it. That is what counts" (Frank Gaebelein, *The Pattern of God's Truth,* Oxford University Press, p. 97).

You can know that you have eternal life. The time is now that the spiritually dead hear the voice of Christ, come alive, and enter into relationship with Him. While the new birth is a great mystery, the process is simple. "Truly, truly, I say to you, he who hears My Word and believes Him who sent Me, has eternal life" (v. 24).

The claim of Christ is that He is the giver of life. One who receives this life will not come into judgment, but "has passed out of death into life" (v. 24). The verb tenses indicate that when a person enters into this process, it remains his.

During my high school years, my faith wavered at times, but

the fact remained that I was changed. I was re-created, redirected. This happens only through Christ who said, "I am the way, and the truth, and the life; no one comes to the Father, but through Me" (14:6).

> And He gave Him authority to execute judgment, because He is the Son of man. Do not marvel at this; for an hour is coming, in which all who are in the tombs shall hear His voice, and shall come forth; those who did the good deeds to a resurrection of life; those who committed the evil deeds to a resurrection of judgment (5:27-29).

A bugler stands at the edge of a graveyard and plays reveille, but nothing happens. He can travel to Arlington National Cemetery and play beside the graves of the brave, but nothing will happen. The dead need a greater authority to bring them to life, the authority in the voice of Christ: "For an hour is coming, when all who are in the tombs shall hear His voice" (v. 28).

The voice of Christ will call believers and unbelievers to resurrection. Will it be like when He called Lazarus from the dead? Will He say, "Kent Hughes, come forth"? Or will it be a general call? It has been said that it is good He specified Lazarus, or the whole graveyard would have emptied! Perhaps Christ will use music. We know a trumpet will sound (1 Cor. 15:52).

Will the bodies of those long dead be "beamed" into existence? Or will the bones take on sinew and skin, as we read in Ezekiel? All we are told is that we will receive new bodies that can experience the fullness of what we have tasted on earth.

At the end of *The Last Battle*, Aslan talks to Peter, Edmund, and Lucy. He tells them that they are dead as the result of a railroad accident:

> And as He [Aslan] spoke, He no longer looked to them like a lion; but the things that began to happen after that were so great and beautiful that I cannot write them. And for us this is the end of

all the stories, and we can most truly say that they all lived happily ever after. But for them it was only the beginning of the real story. All their life in this world and all their adventures in Narnia had only been the cover and title page. Now at last they were beginning chapter 1 of the Great Story which no one on earth has read, which goes on forever; in which every chapter is better than the one before (C.S. Lewis, The Bodley Head, pp. 183-184).

This promise is true for those who believe. Christ's authoritative voice will call us forth to a new life for which life on earth has been but the cover and the title page.

Christ Is Judge

Christ also will have authority to preside in judgment. "And He gave Him authority to execute judgment, because He is the Son of man" (v. 27). In this statement, Jesus reached back to the Book of Daniel for the phrase "Son of man" and identified Himself with it. That title is beautiful and gracious in its context in Daniel (7:13) where the destruction of the bestial empires of the world is followed by the coming of the "Son of man" who sets up a humane, gentle government. Jesus used the term to tell believers that the One who comes in judgment will be like the Son of man. He was reminding them of the Messiah's humanity and the resulting understanding and sympathy He would bring to His own.

Yet the One who is so precious to those who believe will bring terror to those who do not believe. At the Great White Throne Judgment, unbelievers will look into the face of the Man who misses nothing. He will know everything about them, and will have all power over them: "For not even the Father judges anyone, but He has given all judgment to the Son" (v. 22).

Christ was the fleshly expression of Ezekiel's vision—and much more. Many years after Christ's death, the Apostle John had a vision which included four living creatures, a throne with a figure on it, and a rainbow around the throne (Rev. 4:3). The rainbow, as before, calls to mind God's faithfulness and grace but the description of the figure is different. "He who was sitting was like a jasper stone and a sardius in appearance." The jasper and the red of the sardius symbolize the sacrifice of Christ's life. Jesus claimed to be God! His death, resurrection, and final exaltation prove it.

Christ's three mighty claims are established forever. He is identical in action with the Father; He has power to give life; and He has authority to judge:

> That all may honor the Son, even as they honor the Father. He who does not honor the Son does not honor the Father who sent Him (John 5:23).

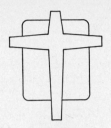

15
Profiting from God's Word

Dr. E.V. Rieu was one of the world's great classical scholars. He was sixty years old and an agnostic when he completed his translation of *Homer* for the Penguin Classic series. The publishing house soon approached Dr. Rieu again, this time asking that he translate the Gospels into English. When Rieu's son heard of the offer, he remarked, "It is going to be interesting to see what Father will make of the four Gospels. It will be even more interesting to see what the four Gospels make of Father." He did not have to wonder long. Within a year his father responded to the message of the Gospels, became a Christian, and joined the church (J.B. Phillips, *The Ring of Truth*, Macmillan, pp. 74-75).

In the Book of Hebrews we read, "For whatever God says to us is full of living power: it is sharper than the sharpest dagger, cutting swift and deep into our innermost thoughts and desires with all their parts" (4:12, TLB). Dr. Rieu discovered that the Scriptures were truly living and powerful and sharper than a two-edged sword. The Word of God pierced his very being, performing divine surgery and giving him life.

Yet many who read the Bible do not experience this impact.

Some scholars spend their lives studying the Word of God but never know its transforming power. While this is a contemporary problem, people of all ages have experienced it. In Jesus' time most of the religious leaders, scholars of the Word, rejected the true interpretation of the Scriptures. Jesus talked with the Pharisees about their handling of the Word of God. Consider His words in terms of their approach, motive, belief, and response.

Approach to the Word

Jesus said to them, "You search the Scriptures, because you think that in them you have eternal life" (John 5:39). The Pharisees regarded the Scriptures with such esteem that they thought the very parchment and words contained eternal life. Their superstitious reverence for the Word of God led to all manner of eccentric behavior. Each letter of the Hebrew alphabet was given a numerical equivalent. Each word had its numerical equivalent. Each line formed a mathematical equation. The scribes even numbered the center letter of each line of Scripture, the center letter in each book, and the center letter in the Old Testament (Sir Frederic Kenyon, *Our Bible and the Ancient Manuscripts,* fifth revised edition, Harper, p. 38).

In copying the Scriptures, a scribe was not allowed to write more than one letter before looking back to the text. This extreme requirement, while resulting in a highly accurate transmission of the Scriptures, points to an underlying fault in the focus of their faith. They really believed that they would find life within the written Word.

One of the greatest rabbis, Hillel, talked about this in a list of maxims:

> More flesh, more worms;
> More wealth, more care;
> More maidservants, more lewdness;
> More menservants, more thieving;

More women, more witchcraft;
More Torah, more life.
Whoso hath gained a good name, has gained it for himself.
Whoso hath gained the words of the Torah,
hath gained for himself life in the world to come.

(Pirke Aboth 2:8)

The Jews believed this so firmly that some of them linked Scripture and memorization of it with salvation. When Jesus said, "You search the Scriptures" (v. 39), He chose a technical word that had been used to describe the extreme studiousness of the scribes and others who labored over the Scriptures at Qumran. Though they always had their noses in the Bible, they never got beyond the parchment and ink. The biblical scholars of the day rejected Jesus when He came to them.

Imagine that you are standing on the observation floor of the John Hancock building overlooking the city of Chicago, just as the sun is setting. You are enjoying the beauty of the sun on the lake when someone tugs on your sleeve. You turn to see a man standing next to you. He says, "Isn't this a wonderful window! Do you see how it is set in steel and how the glass is tinted?"

As he unfolds his pocketknife and begins to scrape a corner of the window, he offers: "I am going to do a chemical analysis of the window; if you will give me your name and phone number, I will call you and let you know what the window is made of."

Naturally you think the man a bit strange, because he has missed the purpose of the window—to view the sunset and the city.

Beyond the Book

While I am committed to detailed study of the Word of God, I do not believe this study is only for the sake of literary analysis, or culling details and statistics. The Bible is the "window" through which we look to see the realities of Christ.

It is possible for us to make the same mistake that the scribes and Pharisees of Jesus' day made. In some homes a family Bible is used for two purposes: to record family events such as births, marriages, and deaths, and to press flowers. It is regarded as a holy book, but is never read or seriously considered. The other, and more likely, possibility in our day is that we will get caught up in the minutiae of the Word. When I was in seminary, I developed a taste for study that has not left me. I like the feel of a Greek New Testament. I can be transported by a critical commentary. Often when I pick up a book, I savor its aroma, but I know that this tendency can be carried to an extreme. I remember long and serious discussions with friends about minutiae. The danger in this is the trivialization of our faith.

In one respect, we should approach the Scriptures like the rabbis who poured over the texts. We need intense study. Each Christian, regardless of occupation, should constantly work at knowing the Bible.

Dr. Harry A. Ironside who ministered so mightily at Moody Church in Chicago for many years did not study formally beyond high school. He did, however, read a lot. A key to his great power is found in this quotation from a biographical sketch:

Under his mother's guidance Harry began to memorize Scripture when he was three. By age fourteen he had read through the Bible fourteen times, once for each year. During the rest of his life he read the Bible through at least once each year (Warren Wiersbe, *Listening to the Giants,* Baker, p. 198).

Once when Ironside and another pastor were speakers at a conference, the two began to discuss their devotional lives. The pastor told Dr. Ironside what he had read for his devotions that morning, and then asked the venerable preacher what he had read. Ironside hesitated and then said, "Well, I read the Book of Isaiah." He was saturated with the Word of God. It is said that he read himself blind, and most of his reading was in the Word of God.

Dr. Stephen Olford commented that many of the great preachers of this century have a Plymouth Brethren background. I asked why this was. Dr. Olford replied that the Plymouth Brethren immerse themselves in their English Bible. Today it is possible for a student to finish seminary and not know the Bible.

We should be people of the Book. Unlike the rabbis, we should come to the Scriptures without preconceived programs and techniques to force on God's Word. We must go beyond the framework and look to Christ. When we see principles, we need to apply them to our lives.

Wrong Motives
The Pharisees studied the Scriptures with wrong motives:

> "I do not receive glory from men; but I know you, that you do not have the love of God in yourselves. I have come in My Father's name, and you do not receive Me; if another shall come in his own name, you will receive him. How can you believe, when you receive glory from one another, and you do not seek the glory that is from the one and only God?" (vv. 41-44)

These educated men who listened to Christ fell short of believing because they were motivated by self-glory rather than by a desire for God's glory. They wanted acclaim from other scholars, and so would line themselves up against one another, as they argued about words. In the rabbinical schools, the study of Scripture was a means to show off intellectual prowess, a way to gain fame. Even the clothing of biblical scholars was distinctive so that they would be recognized. They prayed so as to command attention. People gave them deference and preference. Though they knew the Word of God backward and forward, they were still lost.

Jesus told them that the love of God was not in their hearts. What then did they love? They loved their own opinions about the Word of God, and that love kept them from the love of God.

They had succumbed to the temptation that confronts all of us—to seek our own glory and enshrine our own opinions.

Jesus told them that another would come in His name and that they would receive that one. Subsequent historical accounts tell us that no less than sixty-three messianic claimants attracted followers. People followed them because their claims corresponded with the desires of men. They offered easy victory, political power, and material advantage. Christ offered the Cross.

The self-glorification of the Pharisees was essentially a moral problem. In this text, it is illustrated by their desire to vaunt themselves in their study of the Scriptures, but it touched every part of their lives.

The temptation to self-glorification is just as great today. Even a brief look at German theology in the eighteenth and nineteenth centuries shows men holding to theories about the Scripture, just as the rabbis did. In so doing, German theologians missed the truth. Hermann Reimarus presented a Jesus who was stripped of all supernatural quality. David Friedrich Strauss rejected most of the Gospel as myth. Bruno Bauer denied the historical Jesus. These men studied the Scriptures and missed the message. Their motives made it impossible to find life in Christ.

> Whatever light man finds they doubt it,
> They love not light, but talk about it.
> (John Masefield, *The Everlasting Mercy,*
> Sidgwick and Jackson, p. 47)

It is not only the motive of glorifying self that can keep us from the truth. Any moral deficiency is capable of doing this, for finding the truth is as much a matter of the heart as it is of the mind. A person says, "I've read the Bible and want to believe, but I can't." Further conversation may reveal that this person is having an affair. He cannot believe when he is in that state. Nor can the woman who has an unforgiving spirit and claims she can't believe: Jesus said that we are to forgive as we have been forgiven. An unforgiving person is unforgiven.

When we approach the Scriptures, we need to yield our lives and then focus on God—not on self. We do not bring the Scriptures to us; we take ourselves to the Scriptures. When we are self-yielding, the Scriptures will speak to us.

Absence of Belief

The Pharisees faced yet another problem—that of belief:

"Do not think that I will accuse you before the Father; the one who accuses you is Moses, in whom you have set your hope. For if you believed Moses, you would believe Me; for he wrote of Me. But if you do not believe his writings, how will you believe My words?" (5:45-47)

The purpose of the Law of Moses was to reveal man's need, his sinfulness. At the end of his life, Moses called the Levites together and delivered to them the Law: "Take this book of the Law and place it beside the ark of the covenant of the Lord your God that it may remain there as a witness against you (Deut. 31:26).

The Law was a witness against sins. The Ten Commandments were meant to bring people to the end of themselves in order that they might come to the Messiah. If the Pharisees had believed this, they would have responded to Christ, as Philip did (John 1:45). He realized that Jesus was the prophesied Messiah, and he believed. Though the Pharisees would have died for the Scriptures, they did not really believe them.

Response to the Word

John Broadus was one of the great men in American church history. He resigned from the presidency of the University of Virginia to found the Southern Baptist Seminary in Louisville,

Kentucky. His work was interrupted by the Civil War, and when he returned to Louisville, he had only seven students, yet he was a committed teacher and wrote one of our greatest books on homiletics—for a blind student in his class.

Three weeks before he died, Broadus was before his class. The Scripture reading for that day was Acts 18:24: "Now a certain Jew named Apollos, an Alexandrian by birth, an eloquent man, came to Ephesus and he was mighty in the Scriptures."

Broadus went on to say, "Gentlemen, we must be like Apollos, mighty in the Scriptures." A student later said that a hush fell on that class as Broadus stood and repeated, "mighty in the Scriptures, mighty in the Scriptures, *mighty in the Scriptures!*" (A. T. Robertson, *Types of Preachers in the New Testament*, George H. Doran, p. 15)

How do we become mighty in the Scriptures? How do we continue to hear the voice of God through them? An incident in the life of Jesus gives us an answer. As opposition to Him increased, He spoke more often in parables. On one particular day, He gave the mystery parables. After the first one, His disciples asked Him, "Why do You speak to them in parables?" (Matt. 13:10)

"To you it has been granted to know the mysteries of the kingdom of heaven, but to them it has not been granted. For whoever has, to him shall more be given, and he shall have an abundance; but whoever does not have, even what he has shall be taken away from him" (Matt. 13:11).

If we look at the Parable of the Talents (Luke 19:26), we can more fully understand what Jesus meant. He spoke of the person who lost because he did not use what he had. In essence Christ was saying, "If you do not put truth in motion, it will be taken away. If you act on the truth, you will receive more." We need to write this principle in our hearts. When we repeatedly hear the truth but do not respond to it, we can be sure it will be taken away. This is why I fear for the soul of the person who does not know Christ, but can complacently join a congregation, hear the truths, and never respond; the time will come when he cannot comprehend the truth.

As a believer I am responsible to respond to the truths of the Word of God. When I am moved by something I hear, I write a memorandum to myself so that I will be sure to put into action the truth I have received.

All of us are called to look beyond the window to the Christ that it frames and to respond in belief. Of the Scriptures, Dr. E. V. Rieu wrote: "These words bear the seal of the Son of man and of God and they are the Magna Carta of the human spirit" (J.B. Phillips, *The Ring of Truth,* p. 75).

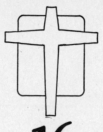

16
Supplier or Saviour?

The people loved it! Here was a Man who could do anything! Out of five barley loaves and two fish He produced enough food to feed 5,000 men, plus women and children, and have twelve baskets left over. What a magnificent king He would make! Already they could see His image instead of Caesar's on their coins, and their feet on the necks of the imperial Roman legion. Verses 14 and 15 record the people's reaction and the response of Jesus.

> When therefore the people saw the sign which He had performed, they said: "This is of a truth the Prophet who is to come into the world." Jesus therefore perceiving that they were intending to come and take Him by force, to make Him king, withdrew again to the mountain by Himself alone (John 6:14-15).

To further disperse the crowd, Jesus sent His disciples by boat to the other side of the Sea of Galilee. When they were out on the lake, a great storm came up and the men were frightened. As they helplessly battled the storm, the Lord walked on the water and said to them, "It is I. Do not be afraid" (vv. 16-25).

The next day the multitudes were still looking for Jesus, wanting to make Him king. When they noticed that one of the boats was gone, they ran around to the other side of the lake looking for Him. They knew He hadn't sailed in the boat with His disciples and their question was, "Rabbi, when did You get here?" (v. 25)

Instead of feeling flattered that they still followed Him, Jesus replied, "Truly, truly, I say to you, you seek Me, not because you saw signs, but because you ate of the loaves, and were filled" (v. 26).

"You are following Me because of the things I have given you. You want a material Saviour." A most contemporary idea.

Rice Christians

An older missionary couple who have served many years in Africa wrote with some sadness about how another group of missionaries were giving the people more material benefits than they and their colleagues were:

> Some of the people are unhappy with us. They want us to do more for them. The other missionaries have no such problem. They use their money to "buy" our people. It puts us in an unpleasant situation when we run into that. It is almost impossible to explain to our Christians why we do not hand out things. We trust we can be of help to our friends.

Missionaries long have talked about "rice Christians"; however, the term doesn't apply just to people in Third World countries. Anyone can be a rice Christian, believing whatever will bring the most benefit for himself. In contrast the Bible presents examples of people who were asked to give up almost everything as a test of their faith. Two of them were Job and Abraham. They did not have a rice faith.

Job

Job was a man of great wealth, integrity, and spirituality. He offered sacrifices daily for his children, in case they had sinned against the Lord. Because Job was so pleasing to God, Satan appeared before God and suggested that Job's piety was nothing more than exchange for material blessings.

"Does Job fear God for nothing? Hast Thou not made a hedge about him and all that he has, on every side? Thou hast blessed the work of his hands, and his possessions have increased in the land. But put forth Thy hand now and touch all that he has; he will surely curse Thee to Thy face" (Job 1:9-11).

God's reply to Satan was, "Behold, all that he has is in your power, only do not put forth your hand on him" (v. 12).

Not long after this, while Job's children were at the home of the eldest son celebrating a birthday, a messenger came to Job's house and told him that the Sabeans had come and taken all of his donkeys and oxen and killed all of Job's servants except himself.

Before Job could digest the meaning of those losses, another messenger arrived to say, "The fire of God had fallen from heaven and burned up your sheep and the herdsmen, and I alone have escaped to tell you" (v. 16, TLB).

As Job was reeling from this second great loss, a third messenger arrived: "Three bands of Chaldeans have driven off your camels and killed your servants, and I alone have escaped to tell you" (v. 17, TLB).

Within a few moments, Job suffered the loss of all that had taken him years to accumulate. As he viewed yet another messenger running toward his house, he must have trembled. He listened and heard that his children who were dining and drinking together in celebration had been killed when the house collapsed from a strong wind (v. 19). Job's response to this final tragedy is astounding:

Then Job arose and tore his robe and shaved his head, and he fell to the ground and worshiped. . . . "Naked I came from my mother's womb, and naked I shall return there. The Lord gave and the Lord has taken away. Blessed be the name of the Lord" (vv. 20-21).

In the moment of his profound loss and sorrow, his first thought was to worship God.

Again Satan and his emissaries came before God to discuss Job's health:

"Skin for skin! Yes, all that a man has he will give for his life. However, put forth Thy hand, now, and touch his bone and his flesh; he will curse Thee to Thy face." So the Lord said to Satan, "Behold, he is in your power, only spare his life." Then Satan went out from the presence of the Lord, and smote Job with sore boils from the sole of his foot to the crown of his head. And he took a potsherd to scrape himself while he was sitting among the ashes. Then his wife said to him, "Do you still hold fast your integrity? Curse God and die!" But he said to her, "You speak as one of the foolish women speaks. Shall we indeed accept good from God and not accept adversity?" (Job. 2:4-10)

In effect Job was saying, "My God is worth serving, even when He takes away my wealth and my health."

Abraham

When Abraham was called by God to leave his home, he obeyed and traveled to an unknown country (Gen. 12). He stopped in Haran until his father, Terah, died and then followed God's call to Palestine, where God promised to make of him a great nation.

In obedience to the word of God, Abraham traveled the length of Palestine through the Gaza Strip, down and back. When it became apparent that he might never have what God had promised—a son, a nation, a Messiah—Abraham must have wondered what God was doing. We can imagine a conversation between Abraham and God sounding something like this:

"God, I have no nation."

"You are going to have one son by the name of Isaac who is going to have two sons named Jacob and Esau. Jacob is going to have twelve sons and they will father a great nation."

"When will that be?"

"Five hundred years."

"But, there is no Messiah. When. . . ?"

"Two thousand years, Abraham."

"And my land for the kingdom—the Promised Land. When is that going to be?"

"Five hundred years."

"Lord, I have given up all of these things! What do You give to me?"

"What do I have to give you? Do not fear, Abram. For I am a shield to you; Your reward shall be very great" (Gen. 15:1).

"Though I have not given you all of these things, what I give you is Myself. I am in the process of giving you Myself."

"It is enough."

Jesus the Bread of Life

When Jesus fed the people bread and fish, He was performing a miracle reminiscent of God providing manna in the wilderness centuries before. In His provision, Jesus was claiming power to supply the peoples' every need—especially their spiritual needs—but they did not understand because their perspective was focused on the material. They asked for yet another sign from Jesus:

> "What then do You do for a sign, that we may see, and believe You? What work do You perform? Our fathers ate the manna in the wilderness; as it is written, 'He gave them bread out of heaven to eat' " (John 6:30-31).

In the following verses, known as the Bread of Life Discourse, Jesus told them plainly that He was the Bread of Life:

Jesus therefore said to them, "Truly, truly, I say to you, it is not Moses who has given you the bread out of heaven, but it is My Father who gives you the true bread out of heaven. For the bread of God is that which comes down out of heaven, and gives life to the world." They said therefore to Him, "Lord, evermore give us this bread." Jesus said to them, "I am the Bread of Life; he who comes to Me shall not hunger, and he who believes in Me shall never thirst" (vv. 32-35).

Jesus here offered Himself as the Bread of Life. The crowd wanted a material sign, but He offered Himself, and that they would not accept.

Origen, the Alexandrian philosopher, makes a comment which is apropos to this materialistic preference, though his comment is on the Scripture dealing with Pilate's question to the crowd: "Whom do you want me to release to you? Barabbas or Jesus who is called the Christ?" As Origen was looking through an ancient manuscript of Matthew 27:16-17, he found a notation saying that Barabbas' name was Jesus—Jesus Barabbas. Origen said, "Jesus Barabbas means son of *a* father. Jesus Christ is Son of *the* Father." Pilate gave the people a choice between the son of *a* father and the Son of *the* Father—between a folk hero and the Messiah. The people chose Barabbas and the hope of material benefits. We are offered the same choice as were the people of Jesus' time, and still many opt for temporary gain.

In the present story, the people likewise rejected Jesus, as our text records:

"But I said to you, that you have seen Me, and yet do not believe" (v. 36). The Jews, therefore, were grumbling about Him, because He said, "I am the bread that came down out of heaven." And they were saying, "Is not this Jesus, the son of

Joseph, whose father and mother we know? How does He now say, 'I have come down out of heaven'?" (vv. 41-42)

Only twenty-four hours earlier, these same people wanted to take Jesus by force as their king, because He had multiplied the loaves. But now as He spoke of spiritual realities, they said, "Who does He think He is?"

It is true that God often blesses believers materially, but it is false to say that if we receive Christ and commit our lives to Him, we will have material wealth and guaranteed good health. Some wrongly teach this, and even claim that if we are not doing well financially or if we are in poor health, we are probably not right with God.

Some have gone so far as to make this false teaching part and parcel of their gospel. This, however, is not the Gospel of Christ. A mix of this philosophy with Christianity is very popular, and many turn to God believing that He will bless them materially and grant them good health. Jesus' promise is that He will give us Himself. In the hardships, the difficult times, in the wonderful exalted moments, and in our gains—in all of these, Jesus is giving Himself to us.

Believing Is Receiving
How do we take the Bread of Life?

"Do not work for the food which perishes, but for the food which endures to eternal life, which the Son of man shall give to you, for on Him the Father, even God, has set His seal." They said therefore to Him, "What shall we do, that we may work the works of God?" Jesus answered and said to them, "This is the work of God, that you believe in Him whom He has sent" (vv. 27-29).

God requires us to believe on Him. The basis of all our works is belief and reception of Him. It is the essential work, as verses 57-58 make so clear:

"As the Living Father sent Me, and I live because of the Father, so he who eats Me, he also shall live because of Me. This is the bread which came down out of heaven; not as the fathers ate, and died; he who eats this bread shall live forever."

Jesus is saying that we receive spiritual bread the same way we receive physical bread—by taking it into ourselves. In his book *Addresses on the Gospel of John,* the late Dr. Harry Ironside wrote, "When we recognize that His precious blood poured out on the cross has atoned for our sins, then we are eating His flesh and drinking His blood" (Loizeaux Brothers, p. 264).

The New Testament phrase, "believe in Christ," includes the idea of interacting with Him. When we believe, we enter into spiritual realities symbolized by His flesh and blood. He becomes our sustenance. His life becomes our life so we experience the reality of His words, "For apart from Me you can do nothing" (John 15:5). We realize that when we have Jesus, we have everything.

Most of the people of Jesus' day were not ready to receive Him as the Bread of Life. "Many therefore of His disciples, when they heard this said, 'This is a difficult statement; who can listen to it?' " (6:60)

We read that many of Jesus' disciples no longer followed Him once they understood what He was really about. And then we have some of the most poignant words in all of Scripture: "Jesus said therefore to the Twelve, 'You do not want to go away also, do you?' " (6:67)

This was the man who could do anything. And yet He didn't. And He doesn't, so that we may come to know Him. Jesus wants us to experience more and more of who He is, instead of focusing on material benefits.

17
God's Children in Life's Storms

Jesus' disciples were in trouble, and all because they had pointed their boat in the direction Jesus had told them to go. After He had fed the 5,000, He had told His disciples to cross the sea to Capernaum. Jesus *made* them cross in a boat (Matt. 14:22). The word *made* can also be translated "compelled or forced." Jesus may have given the boat a shove to get them started in the right direction.

They were several miles from shore, it was dark, and the sea was churning from a strong wind. The great preacher Clarence Macartney described it this way:

> Peter, no doubt, took command; and you can see him there holding the tiller with his stalwart arm, and his beard annointed with the foam of the sea, as in stentorian tones he commands the disciples to trim the ship, lower the sails, and take to the oars. Where all was calm a little while ago, now all is tummult and confusion. As the tempest rages over the lake, the ship tosses

*Since Matthew provides a more detailed account, both passages should be studied in order to understand the full significance of the story.

like a cork up and down in the great waves, the white foam of the great rollers gleaming in the blackness of the night like the teeth of some monster of the sea (*Great Nights in the Bible,* Abingdon Cokesbury, p. 201).

The disciples were in trouble because they had steered their boat into contrary winds. I believe there is a deeper truth in this. We can get into the storms of life in two ways. One is to run from God's will, as the Prophet Jonah did, or to face contrary winds as followers of Christ. The disciples were in a storm because they had been obedient to God. It is inevitable that followers of Christ will have storms in their lives. It may even seem that God has sent the trouble.

I can relate to their distress at sailing into contrary winds because of a teenage "sailing" experience. In 1958, a high school buddy pulled up in front of my house towing a contraption he called a sailboat. Actually it was a large surfboard with a sail. We took that ill-conceived assemblage down to Newport Bay to try to sail it from one end to the other. We managed to get it rigged up and into the water. Neither of us had sailed before. To reach the point we wanted, we had to sail into the wind. It took us four hours to sail a quarter of a mile, and in that four hours we capsized the boat eight times, the last time in front of a car ferry. When we turned the boat around it took us only ten minutes to return.

The storm was raging around the disciples. The spray was dashing over the boat and the masts had begun to crack. Water was sloshing in the dark hold of the beleaguered ship. The disciples must have wondered, "Has the Lord forgotten us?"

Jesus Sees and Cares

In the parallel passage in Mark, we read that Jesus saw them (6:48). We don't know if He saw the disciples during the lightning or if He saw them through His omniscience, but He saw them. In dark times, we too can be assured that He sees and cares. The psalmist wrote:

> Where can I go from Thy Spirit? Or where can I flee from Thy presence? If I ascend to heaven, Thou art there. If I make my bed in Sheol, behold, Thou. . . . If I take the wings of the dawn, if I dwell in the remotest part of the sea (Ps. 139:7-9).

Wherever we go, the Lord is there, and He knows all the details.

Though Christ saw the disciples helplessly working to right their situation, He delayed in coming to them. We don't know why He delayed, and yet there is a hint in another story in John's Gospel. When Lazarus was on the verge of death, Mary and Martha sent for Jesus to come and heal him. Jesus delayed, allowed Lazarus to die, and then came and raised him up (John 11:1-7). At times He takes us to the very end of our strength and then does for us what we can not do for ourselves.

Jesus Comes in the Darkness

Sometime between three and six (Matt. 14:25), in the darkest part of the night, when the disciples were exhausted, Jesus came to them, walking on the water. You may have experienced that last minute help—the check that arrived just in time, a house that sold at the eleventh hour.

My wife and I experienced that kind of timing when I was in college. During my senior year we were expecting our first child. It was a difficult time in our lives because I was so busy. I was working full time in a factory and taking a full load in school and my take-home pay was $73 a week. I calculated that by the time the baby was born, I could save $160, but the doctor wanted $250 and the hospital wanted $250. I knew I would be far short. My wife and I prayed, for we were in a place of extremity.

When my wife went for her final examination, the doctor looked over her charts and noticed for the first time that I was studying for the ministry. He was not a Christian, and yet he said to Barbara, "I am not going to charge you for the delivery." Wonderful! We needed only the $250 for the hospital.

After our baby was born, when I went to the hospital to pick up my little family, I had $163 in my pocket. I didn't know how it was going to work out, since that wasn't enough to pay the hospital bill. But it was. Our timing had been just right and we had been charged for only two days instead of three. The bill was $160 and I had $3 left to buy flowers for my wife! We truly felt that Jesus had come to us in our dark place and had given the help we needed.

We may know Christ, but we will never know Him deeply until He comes to us during a storm. It was not until Job had suffered the loss of everything that he said, "I have heard of Thee by the hearing of the ear; but now my eye sees Thee" (Job 42:5). It is the difference between hearing about Him and seeing Him for ourselves.

Jesus Is Not Recognized

In telling the story, Matthew wrote, "And when the disciples saw Him walking on the sea, they were frightened, saying, 'It is a ghost!' And they cried out for fear" (Matt. 14:26).

The disciples' reaction was understandable. It was dark, the wind was blowing fiercely, and they were barely hanging on to their lives. They saw an apparition—a water demon—coming across the waters, looking like the Ancient Mariner without his ship! They were terrified.

A perversity in the human heart can cause us to push God away when He comes to us in the storm. One reason for this is that He often comes to us in ways we do not expect, or in ways that we reject—perhaps through a person to whom we feel superior, or through an occupational tragedy, or through a person we have rejected. We tend to say, "No, God! You cannot come to me that way! We need to be careful that we do not, through pride, ignorance, or fear, reject what God is trying to do for us.

As Jesus came closer to the boat, His voice rose above the storm, "It is I; do not be afraid" (John 6:20). At that moment, the disciples' attitude changed 180 degrees. Seconds before, they had feared for their lives; then they heard the voice of Christ. He did not say, "Do not be afraid" until He had identified Himself.

The account in Matthew tells us that Peter called out to Jesus:

"Lord, if it is You, command me to come to You on the water." And He said, "Come!" And Peter got out of the boat, and walked on the water and came toward Jesus (14:28-29).

Deliverance in the Storm

In faith Peter stepped out and began to walk on the water. He sank only when he took his eyes off Jesus and looked around at the water, but Peter knew what to do then. He cried, "Lord, save me!" Then the two walked together to the boat to join the other disciples.

John ends the story this way: "They were willing therefore to receive Him into the boat; and immediately the boat was at the land to which they were going" (John 6:21).

We can be sure that in following Christ we will run into contrary winds, but we can be comforted, knowing that He knows and sees all of our predicaments. He understands the nuances of our thoughts and personalities in a way that no one else can understand.

Are you going through storms of life? Jesus sees you, and you can rejoice that His understanding help is on the way. Expect Him to come to you in the darkest part of the night, and do not ignore or reject Him when He comes. Be open to the work of God in your life. Focus on Him and then let Him into the "boat" with you.

Your storm may be an occupational uncertainty, or unemployment. It may be conflict in your home, or emotional insecurity. It may be conflict with other believers, or an ethical dilemma. The storms will cease, as He provides His answer for you.

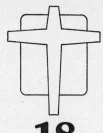

18
Give Us This Bread

In 1930 one of the most famous of living authors was William Somerset Maugham. He was known as a novelist, a playwright, and a master of the short story. His novel, *Of Human Bondage*, was established as a classic, and his play, *The Constant Wife*, had been staged thousands of times.

By 1965, Somerset Maugham was ninety-one years old and fabulously wealthy. Royalties continued to pour in, despite the fact that he had not written a word in years.

Shortly before Maugham's death, he was visited by his nephew, Robin Maugham, who later wrote an article describing the time they had together in his uncle's villa:

I looked round the drawing room at the immensely valuable furniture and pictures and objects that Willie's success had enabled him to acquire. I remembered that the villa itself and the wonderful garden I could see through the windows—a fabulous setting on the edge of the Mediterranean—were worth £600,000. (It cost him £7,000). Willie had eleven servants, including his cook, Annette, who was the envy of all the other millionaires on the Riviera. He dined on silver plates, waited on by Marius, his butler, and Henri, his footman. But it no longer meant anything to him.

The following afternoon, I found Willie reclining on a sofa, peering through his spectacles at a Bible which had very large print. He looked horribly wizened, and his face was grim. "I've been reading the Bible you gave me . . . and I've come across the quotation: 'What shall it profit a man if he gain the whole world and lose his own soul?' I must tell you, my dear Robin, that the text used to hang opposite my bed when I was a child. . . . Of course, it's all a lot of bunk. But the thought is quite interesting all the same."

That evening, in the drawing room after dinner, Willie flung himself down onto the sofa. "O, Robin, I'm so tired. . . ." He gave a gulp and buried his head in his hands. "I've been a failure the whole way through my life," he said. "I've made mistake after mistake. I've made a hash of everything." I tried to comfort him. "You're the most famous writer alive. Surely that means something?" "I wish I'd never written a single word," he answered. "It's brought me nothing but misery. . . . Everyone who's got to know me well has ended up hating me. . . . My whole life has been a failure. . . . And now it's too late to change. It's too late. . . ." Willie looked up, and his grip tightened on my hands. He was staring toward the floor. His face was contorted with fear, and he was trembling violently. Willie's face was ashen as he stared in horror ahead of him. Suddenly, he began to shriek. "Go away!" he cried. "I'm not ready. . . I'm not dead yet. . . I'm not dead yet, I tell you. . . ." His high-pitched, terror-struck voice seemed to echo from wall to wall. I looked round, but the room was empty as before. "There's no one there, Willie." Willie began to gasp hysterically (*London Times,* April 9, 1978).

Though Maugham was one of the most famous and feted men of his generation, when it was time for the reckoning, he found his life empty and worthless. He was afraid to die.

This is not what God intends life to be. He wants to rescue us from empty lives and to give us freedom. Jesus saw the people of His time headed in the same direction as was Maugham. He wanted to free them, but He had to show them their emptiness before they were ready to receive the satisfaction He alone offers.

Lifting Their Sights

The crowds pursued Jesus because He had supplied them with material benefits, but they failed to see Him as One who could supply their spiritual needs as well. Jesus knew they needed their sights lifted:

> Jesus answered them and said, "Truly, truly, I say to you, you seek Me, not because you saw signs, but because you ate of the loaves, and were filled. Do not work for the food which perishes, but for the food which endures to eternal life, which the Son of man shall give to you, for on Him the Father, even God, has set His seal" (John 6:26-27).

The people asked Jesus what work they could do to obtain the eternal bread. Jesus told them spiritual food does not come by work; it is given by the Son of man. They were to believe in the One God sent (vv. 28-29). Instead of understanding what Jesus was teaching them, the people pressed for more proof:

> They said therefore to Him, "What then do You do for a sign, that we may see, and believe You? What work do You perform? Our fathers ate the manna in the wilderness; as it is written, 'He gave them bread out of heaven to eat' " (vv. 30-31).

In effect they said, "Jesus, You did a great sign yesterday when You fed the 5,000, but we want You to do a miracle on a par with Moses' miracle. He fed all of Israel six days a week for forty years, with bread from heaven."

To understand what they had in mind, we have to look back to the Book of Exodus.

Then they set out from Elim, and all the congregation of the sons of Israel came to the wilderness of Sin, which is between Elim and Sinai, on the fifteenth day of the second month after their departure from the land of Egypt. And the whole congregation of the sons of Israel grumbled against Moses and Aaron in the wilderness. And the sons of Israel said to them, "Would that we had died by the Lord's hand in the land of Egypt, when we sat by the pots of meat, when we ate bread to the full; for you have brought us out into this wilderness to kill this whole assembly with hunger." Then the Lord said to Moses, "Behold, I will rain bread from heaven for you; and the people shall go out and gather a day's portion every day, that I may test them, whether or not they will walk in My instruction" (16:1-4).

And the Lord spoke to Moses, saying, "I have heard the grumblings of the sons of Israel; speak to them, saying, 'At twilight, you shall eat meat, and in the morning you shall be filled with bread; and you shall know that I am the Lord your God.' " So it came about at evening that the quails came up and covered the camp, and in the morning, there was a layer of dew around the camp. When the layer of dew evaporated, behold, on the surface of the wilderness there was a fine flake-like thing, fine as the hoarfrost on the ground. When the sons of Israel saw it, they said to one another, "What is it?" For they did not know what it was. And Moses said to them, "It is the bread which the Lord has given you to eat" (vv. 11-15).

We Will Believe If . . .

The crowds of Jesus' day were telling Him that if He would produce manna from heaven, as in the day of Moses, they would believe. They were as forgetful as we are of God's provision of yesterday. They wanted another miracle before they would follow Him. Jesus replied:

"Truly, truly, I say to you, it is not Moses who has given you the bread out of heaven, but it is My Father who gives you the true bread out of heaven. For the bread of God is that which comes down out of heaven, and gives life to the world" (John 6:32-33).

As the people began to understand that He was speaking of something beyond the material, they said, "Lord, evermore give us this bread" (v. 34).

Jesus had brought them to the point where He could present Himself as the food they sought: "I am the Bread of Life; he who comes to Me shall not hunger, and he who believes in Me shall never thirst" (v. 35).

It is no coincidence that Jesus was born in Bethlehem, the City of Bread, or that John speaks of the Word becoming flesh which was broken by men.

Several similarities exist between manna and Jesus, the Bread of Life. The manna typified Jesus in that it was white like fallen snow, just as Christ was without blemish. Manna was also accessible. When a man walked outside of camp to gather it, he had the choice of treading on it or picking it up and gathering it to himself. We can either tread on Jesus or we can take Him to ourselves.

Jesus is the Bread of Life. He is our sustenance, and those who come to Him shall not hunger or thirst. Apart from Christ, nothing provides lasting satisfaction. The best of fishing trips must be followed by another fishing trip, the best racquetball game by another game. We can eat a great dinner and yet soon need another. We can wear clothes by Halston, but we will have to buy new clothes eventually.

Dressed in his finest garb, night after night, Somerset Maugham ate and drank with the most famous people in the world, yet nothing satisfied him.

Satisfied With Christ

In contrast, Dietrich Bonhoeffer finished his life satisfied with Christ. When he was transferred from the Nazi prison to the main Gestapo prison in 1944, Bonhoeffer calmly said good-bye to his friends in prison. They later said that he seemed at peace, except that "his eyes were quite unnatural." One of the last messages received from him bore testimony to his marvelous spirit. It was a poem entitled, "New Year 1945." The third stanza reads:

> Should it be ours to drain the cup of grieving
> even to the dregs of pain, at Thy command,
> we will not falter, thankfully receiving
> all that is given by Thy loving hand.
> (*Cost of Discipleship,* Macmillan, p. 20)

Jesus therefore said to them, "Truly, truly, I say to you, unless you eat the flesh of the Son of man and drink His blood, you have no life in yourselves." (v. 53). When Christ spoke of the people partaking of Him as they would of bread they questioned, "How do we do that?" The same question is asked today, and the answer is that we must live as if Christ is the greatest reality.

> Is He as real to you spiritually as something you can taste or handle? Is He as much a part of you as that which you eat? Do not think me blasphemous when I say that He must be as real and as useful to you as a hamburger and french fries. I say this because, though He is obviously far more real and useful than these; the unfortunate thing is that for many people He is much less (James Boice, *The Gospel of John—An Expositional Commentary,* Vol. 2, Zondervan, p. 219).

Is Christ as substantially real to us as the bread we eat? Bread is indispensable. It was difficult for an ancient man to conceive of living without bread, for it was a symbol of life. We claim to have the Bread of Life, but is Christ indispensable to us?

Partaking of Christ

In her book *Smoke on the Mountain,* Joy Davidman commented on the first commandment, "Thou shalt have no other gods before Me," by turning it around to say, "Thou shalt have Me." Jesus said, "I am the Bread of Life. Partake of Me."

Bread is eaten daily. In a week, most of us eat twenty-one meals, plus snacks. In that time, how often do we partake of the Bread of Life? Our schedules betray us as we find ourselves spending so little time with Christ. He wants to give us Himself, but that demands partaking of Him regularly; making Him part of our lives.

Somerset Maugham's tragedy was dramatized in the moment he took the Bible in his wrinkled hands and read, "What shall it profit a man if he gain the whole world and lose his own soul?" What if he had read more and opened himself to the Bread of Life? Perhaps he would have been satisfied.

Perhaps you yearn to be satisfied and are thinking, "I want this Bread of Life, but I don't know how to get it any more than the people of Jesus' day did." You hope some good work you are doing will win you the satisfaction you seek. Jesus said, "This is the work of God, that you believe in Him whom He has sent" (John 6:29).

If you believe and partake of the Bread of Life, through His Word and in prayer, you will be satisfied. Christ will change your life.

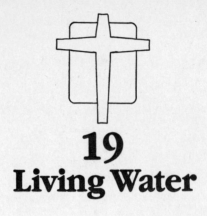

19
Living Water

The Feast of Booths or Tabernacles took place after all of the harvest had been gathered. This joyous celebration was well-attended for two reasons: it was an exciting festival, and it was one of three festivals required of every Jewish male who lived within twenty miles of Jerusalem.

If such a happening were to take place today, we might call it The Jerusalem Camping and Recreational Vehicle Convention. Shelters sprang up in the most unlikely places—on flat rooftops, in dark alleys, and even in the courts of the temple. All of the shelters conformed to the rabbinical building code. Walls were constructed so that light came through, as a reminder to the Jews of their journey in the wilderness. The roof had to show enough sky so that the stars could be seen. The shelters were to be a yearly reminder to the people of their wanderings in the wilderness and of God's provisions for them.

The Feast of Tabernacles was called "the season of our gladness." The people dressed in their Sabbath best for the festive week. To the Prophet Zechariah the Feast was a symbol of the future, of a golden age to come in which there would be a universal Feast of Tabernacles (Zech. 14).

At the heart of the celebration was a daily rite which we need to be aware of in order to understand John 7. Rabbinical literature tells us that each morning great multitudes gathered at the Temple of Herod, carrying a citrus fruit called an ethrog in their left hands. The ethrog was a reminder of the land to which God had brought them and of the bountiful blessings they had enjoyed. In their right hands they carried a lulab, which was a combination of three trees—a palm, a willow, and a myrtle—emblematic of the stages of their ancestors' journey through the wilderness.

Each morning the people would gather with the ethrog and the lulab. The crowds followed the priest who carried a golden pitcher to the Pool of Siloam, chanting psalms and waving their lulabs in rhythm. As they approached the Pool, the priest would dip his pitcher into the water and the people would say, "Therefore you will joyously draw water from the springs of salvation" (Isa. 12:3). The crowd then marched back to the temple, entering the Water Gate to the blast of the priests' trumpets. The priest who had led them circled the altar once, and with accompanying priests ascended to the platform, and poured out the water.

Back in Galilee

While all this was going on in Jerusalem, Jesus had remained at home in Galilee. He was unwilling to walk in Judea because the Jews were seeking to kill Him (John 7:1). Jesus' brothers had also stayed at home and John reports a conversation which took place:

> His brothers therefore said to Him, "Depart from here, and go into Judea, that Your disciples also may behold Your works which You are doing. For no one does anything in secret, when he himself seeks to be known publicly. If You do these things, show Yourself to the world" (vv. 3-4).

The reason for their contemptuous tone is that they did not believe in Him. Do you sense the situation in which Jesus found Himself? The Jews in Jerusalem wanted to kill Him and now His brothers were urging Him to go to the celebration at the risk of His life.

It is important to understand Jesus' reply to His brothers: "My time is not yet at hand; but your time is always opportune" (v. 6). The word Jesus used for time is *kairos*, a word which often carries the idea for opportunity. What He said to them was, "I want you to understand that the right psychological moment is not here, and I am waiting for that moment." Though our Lord seemed to be pushed by all those around Him, He was in complete control.

Jesus was up to something big. Aside from the Cross, the moment that lay before Him was the most dramatic of His life. After their conversation, Jesus' brothers went up to Jerusalem to the feast, while He stayed behind. Yet, shortly after they left, He too went to Jerusalem "not publicly, but as it were, in secret" (v. 10). Without His disciples or family traveling with Him, He could go unrecognized.

"The Jews therefore were seeking Him at the feast, and were saying, 'Where is He?' " (v. 11) The Jewish leaders were continually asking, "Where is He?" They wanted to put Jesus to death. Even the multitudes reflected tension:

And there was much grumbling among the multitudes concerning Him; some were saying, "He is a good man"; others were saying, "No, on the contrary, He leads the multitude astray." Yet no one was speaking openly of Him for fear of the Jews (vv. 12-13).

The controversies that raged about who Jesus was and what His powers were went on behind closed doors. Outside discussions were carried on in hushed tones.

When Jesus arrived at the temple, He did not try to conceal

Himself; rather, He went in and toward the front where He began to teach. Those hearing Him claimed that they had never heard anyone teach as He did that day, and they questioned Him about His authority. He answered them, "What I have comes from the Father." When He accused them of wanting to kill Him, they retorted that He had a demon and was paranoid. Then Jesus really set things in motion:

> Jesus therefore cried out in the temple, teaching and saying, "You both know Me and know where I am from; and I have not come of Myself, but He who sent Me is true, whom you do not know. I know Him; because I am from Him, and He sent Me" (vv. 28-29).

After this pronouncement, controversy raged (vv. 30-36). Some wanted to seize Him, but others believed as the Feast of Tabernacles progressed toward the final day.

Thirsting

On the seventh and final day of the feast, the priests and people repeated the same ritual described earlier. They came into the temple chanting their psalms, waving their lulabs. As they en tered the Water Gate, the trumpets sounded. But this day was different. On the seventh day, the priest would circle the altar seven times in succession—as the people of Israel had encircled the walls of Jericho. When he came around for the sixth time, he would be joined by another priest carrying the wine. They would ascend the ramp to the altar of holocaust where they were together to pour out the water and wine on the altar. When they were in place, there would come a pause as the priest raised up his pitcher. Always the crowds shouted for him to hold it higher and he would do so. It was considered to be the height of joy in a person's life if he could see the water being poured out onto the altar.

It was on this last and greatest day of the feast that Jesus cried aloud:

"If any man is thirsty, let him come to Me and drink. He who believes in Me, as the Scripture said, 'From his innermost being shall flow rivers of living water' " (vv. 37-38).

Our Lord used an image that had powerful impact in the Middle East. The people there understood thirst.

One of the tragedies of our age is that deep inside we may be thirsting after God and yet interpret that longing as the desire for a new car, an exciting event, a new love. Or we may realize that we thirst for God and yet try to satisfy this in the wrong way. The Prophet Jeremiah wrote:

"For My people have committed two evils: They have forsaken Me, the fountain of living waters, to hew for themselves cisterns, broken cisterns, that can hold no water" (Jer. 2:13).

Somerset Maugham died an unhappy, empty old man—and fearful of death. The reason, I believe, is seen in the final line of his famous autobiography, *The Summing Up:* "The beauty of life is nothing but this; that each should act in conformity with his nature and his business" (Arno, p. 310). He was saying that the beauty of life is nothing but to do your own thing! That brought tragedy to his life.

Jesus encouraged healthy thirst. I am glad that He did not specify anyone's name in His invitation but made it open to every person, saying, "If any man is thirsty. . . ." What a wonderful provision for our spiritual health. To thirst after the water that He gives is to hunger and thirst for all of His righteousness. If I could give one gift, it would be a spiritual hunger and thirst after righteousness, the Holy Spirit, and the Word.

Drinking
We quench our thirst by coming to the Lord who gives freely. No one need wait, anyone can drink of this water—a child, a teenager, an older person, an invalid—anyone.

Though Jesus' offer is open and the water is free, there are terms. These are so well illustrated by C.S. Lewis in *The Silver Chair*. Jill had just seen a lion and was frightened. She ran off into the forest and so wore herself out that she was about to die of thirst, or so she thought. Just then she heard the gurgling of a brook in the distance. She got up and went toward the sound and the brook and was about to take of its water when she saw the lion in front of her. The lion spoke to her:

"Are you not thirsty?" said the Lion.

"I'm *dying* of thirst," said Jill.

"Then drink," said the Lion.

"May I—could I—would you mind going away while I do?" said Jill.

The Lion answered this only by a look and a very low growl. And as Jill gazed at its motionless bulk, she realized that she might as well have asked the whole mountain to move aside for her convenience. The delicious rippling noise of the stream was driving her nearly frantic.

"Will you promise not to—do anything to me, if I do come?" said Jill.

"I make no promise," said the Lion.

Jill was so thirsty now that, without noticing it, she had come a step nearer.

"Do you eat girls?" she said.

"I have swallowed up girls and boys, women and men, kings and emperors, cities and realms," said the Lion. It didn't say this as if it were boasting, nor as if it were sorry, nor as if it were angry. It just said it.

"I daren't come and drink," said Jill.

"Then you will die of thirst," said the Lion.

"Oh, dear!" said Jill, coming another step nearer. "I suppose I must go and look for another stream then."

"There is no other stream," said the Lion.

It never occurred to Jill to disbelieve the Lion—no one who had seen his stern face could do that—and her mind suddenly made itself up. It was the worst thing she had ever had to do, but she went forward to the stream, knelt down, and began scooping up water in her hand. It was the coldest, most refreshing water she had ever tasted (Collins, pp. 26-27).

When we come to the water, we too are coming to a lion—to the Lion of the Tribe of Judah. We come to the water on the Lion's terms and we have to yield ourselves by faith to drink of the water. There is no other stream. You may feel so thirsty for the presence of God in your life that you think you may die without it. You can come to Him in faith and receive the water that refreshes to eternal life.

Living

"He who believes in Me, as the Scripture said, 'From his innermost being shall flow rivers of living water.' " But this He spoke of the Spirit (John 7:38-39).

Jesus tells us of satisfaction in our innermost being. The words *innermost being* are better translated "belly." That part of us which is not easily satisfied, which craves so much, can be satisfied. The innermost self can become the very seat of satisfaction through the Spirit of Christ indwelling our lives.

When we experience this satisfaction, it does more than refresh us. It overflows to others. Notice Christ did not say "river" but "rivers." Rivers of living water flow out of us by virtue of the indwelling Spirit of Christ, when we come to Him and drink of the water. When we truly satisfy our thirst, that satisfaction flows out of us to others. Corrie Ten Boom was such a person. Mother Teresa of Calcutta is another whose testimony is, "Yet not I, but Christ liveth in me" (Gal. 2:20). The satisfaction she finds in Christ overflows to the dying in Calcutta. (Malcolm Muggeridge, *Something Beautiful for God*, Ballantine, p. 4)

A century ago, Billy Bray was a miner in Cornwall. This

dynamic Christian was so effervescent, so overflowing with Christ, that wherever he went, men trusted Christ. Each day as he went down into the mines—which were very dangerous at that time—he would pray with the miners: "Lord, if any of us must be killed or die today, let it be me. Let not one of these men die for they are not happy and I am, and if I die today I shall go to heaven" (J. Gilchrist Lawson, *Deeper Experiences of Famous Christians,* Chicago Glad Tidings Publisher, p. 267).

Those who drink of the Spirit of Christ have powerful and overflowing lives, but they cannot experience this satisfaction until their lives give satisfaction to others.

John Bunyan knew about this. He wrote:

> There was a man,
> The world did think him mad;
> The more he gave away,
> The more he had.

When our lives become slow and stagnant, and we begin to focus on ourselves, the remedy is not to concentrate on our own satisfaction, but rather on the satisfaction of Christ flowing out through us. When we come to a stop in our spiritual lives, we should look for avenues of service. When we drink of the Holy Spirit, He will flow out to others.

The Rock Is Christ

It was during the desert wanderings, which the Feast of Tabernacles portrayed, that Moses came to the rock and smote it, and out of the rock came rivers of living water. The smitten rock is a picture of Christ. The Apostle Paul wrote to the church at Corinth: "All drank the same spiritual drink, for they were drinking from a spiritual rock which followed them; and the rock was Christ" (1 Cor. 10:4).

Jesus referred to Himself as the One from whom they would drink—but not yet, for He had not yet been smitten on the cross and resurrected; therefore, the Spirit had not yet come.

When God instructed Moses in the wilderness to strike the rock, he did, and God provided water. The second time God told Moses to speak to the rock but in his anger at the people, Moses smote the rock again. Water came out for them to drink, but Moses paid heavily for his action.

While his entire life had been committed to the emancipation of his people, he was not allowed to enter the Promised Land. The rock was to be smitten only once. It was a picture of Christ who was stricken only once.

When we come to Christ now, we are to tell Him our need for living water and thus receive the satisfaction which only He can give.

20
The Light of Life

Another great ceremony during the Feast of Tabernacles was the illumination of the temple, which took place in the treasury at the beginning of the feast. It was a spectacular celebration, both in concept and in observance.

In the court of women, which was part of the treasury, was a colonnade with thirteen great treasure chests. The chests were called trumpets because they were shaped like trumpets standing on their faces—narrow at the top and round at the bottom. These trumpets promoted a program of designated giving. The first two were for half-shekels which every Jew had to pay for the upkeep of the temple. The second two were for offerings for pigeons for rites of purification. The fifth trumpet was for wood for sacrifices, the sixth for incense, and the seventh for the upkeep of the golden vessels of the temple. If a person had any money left, the remaining six trumpets were for love offerings, or undesignated giving (William Barclay, *The Gospel of John,* Vol. 2, Westminster, p. 11).

In the center of the treasury were four great candelabra. Some accounts say that these giant torches were as high as the walls of the temple. At the top of these golden candelabra were great bowls that held sixty-five liters of oil. A ladder extended to each candelabra, and when evening came, healthy young priests carried the oil to the top where they lighted the protruding wicks. The resulting flames illumined the whole temple and could be seen in all of Jerusalem.

> Men of piety and good works used to dance before them with burning torches in their hands, singing songs and praises, and countless Levites played on harps, lyres, cymbals, and trumpets and instruments of music (Mishna Sukkah 5:2-3, *The Mishna,* Trans. Herbert Danby, Oxford University Press, p. 180).

The people danced till dawn. This was an exotic festival celebrating the great pillar of fire that led the people of Israel during their sojourn in the wilderness. It was here before these immense extinguished torches that Jesus raised His voice above the crowd and proclaimed, "I am the Light of the World; he who follows Me shall not walk in the darkness, but shall have the light of life" (John 8:12).

There could scarcely be a more dramatic time and place for Jesus to announce one of the supreme truths about Himself. Yet what did He mean by this declaration?

Christ's Claim

Those great torches in the temple symbolized the Shekinah glory. In effect, Christ was reminding the people, "Do you remember the pillar of fire that came between the Israelites and the Egyptians in the Red Sea and protected the Israelites on their wanderings in the wilderness? I am that Light of the World. I am identified with the Shekinah glory!" Jesus was claiming to be God. His identification with that pillar of fire reveals something about His incarnation. Within the cloud that led Israel through the wilderness, was a heart of fire which shone forth at night but was sheathed by day. When our Lord came, He sheathed His glory in flesh so that we might look on

Him. In the Old Testament, God is often called the light. In one of the last verses of the Old Testament we read, "But for you who fear My name, the sun of righteousness will rise with healing in its wings" (Mal. 4:2).

When Simeon took the Baby Jesus in his arms in the temple to bless Him, he sang, "Because of the tender mercy of our God, with which the Sunrise from on high shall visit us, to shine on those who sit in darkness and the shadow of death" (Luke 1:78-79).

When the Apostle John wrote, "We beheld His glory, glory as of the Only Begotten from the Father" (John 1:14), I believe he was referring, at least in part, to the transfiguration of Jesus when His face shone forth as the sun.

In Jesus' statement in the temple, He was not only saying that He is the Light of the World, but that the benefits and comforts in the cloud in the wilderness also came from Him. What a precious truth! He was telling them, "I was the One who protected you. I guided you through the wilderness. I enveloped the tabernacle. I came into the temple of Solomon and filled it with such glory that the priests could not serve. I am the Shekinah glory."

In our dark world, we need to keep this claim of Christ before us. Jesus is the light of life in every way. He is the answer. If you feel that you are stumbling at this point in your life, wondering what it is all about, and you are barely able to take another step, Christ reminds you, "I am the light of life."

Light for Others

Christ promised that those who follow Him "shall not walk in darkness, but shall have the light of life" (v. 12). The Israelites kept their attention on the cloud. They watched its configuration to see when and where it would move. At night they walked in its light. No matter how dark the night, when they were under the luminous cloud, there was no stumbling, no confusion, no fear. Jesus provides similar benefits for those who know Him as the light of life.

Not long ago, I saw a group of people trying to walk an obstacle course blindfolded. Even the smallest obstacle became difficult. It is true in our own darkness that obstacles which should not be great can seem as huge stumbling blocks; but when we have the light of Christ in our lives, we begin to understand how to proceed through life.

In the phrase "shall have the light of life" the key word is *have*. Christ is not only saying that we have the light coming into us, but that we also, in a sense, become a shaft of the Lord's light. The Apostle Paul said, "You were formerly darkness, but now you are light in the Lord" (Eph. 5:8). We share the very light that Jesus Christ shared. Paul told the Philippian Christians that in a dark world they appeared as lights (Phil. 2:15).

Jesus' claim suggests one other wonder that is precious to me personally. At the end of the mystery parables, Jesus made this statement: "The righteous will shine forth as the sun in the kingdom of their Father" (Matt. 13:43). C.S. Lewis once noted that the heavens only reflect the glory of God, but we share the glory of God with Christ and we will be more glorious than the heavens. In *The Weight of Glory,* Lewis wrote:

> Nature is mortal. We shall outlive her. When all the suns and nebulae have passed away, each one of you will still be alive. Nature is only the image, the symbol, but it is a symbol Scripture invites me to use. We are summoned to pass in through nature beyond her to the splendor which she fitfully reflects (Eerdmans, p. 13).

While I don't understand that, I believe it with all my heart. Christians await a glory that involves a shining forth. I don't know if we will be 100 watts or 1,000, but somehow we are to become beings glorious beyond imagination: "We know that, when He appears, we shall be like Him, because we shall see Him just as He is" (1 John 3:2).

John also wrote, "And there shall no longer be any night; and they shall not have need of the light of a lamp nor the light of the sun, because the Lord God shall illumine them; and they shall reign forever and ever" (Rev. 22:5).

Not only will the light be in us, but we have the light to illumine our steps as we walk through life. Light comes into us so that it can go out to others, making us to be light and life to them.

Those Who Reject Him

Not all who heard Christ's claim to be the light of life were pleased. "The Pharisees therefore said to Him, 'You are bearing witness of Yourself; Your witness is not true' " (John 8:13).

They hung their disbelief on a technicality, just as so many people do today who do not *want* to believe in Christ. Within the Hebrew judicial system, truth had to be verified by two witnesses. This is why the Pharisees told Christ that He couldn't establish truth on the basis of His own testimony.

Their hardheartedness reveals to us another reality—that when Jesus is loved and trusted, He becomes light; when He is neglected, He becomes darkness. The wilderness cloud produced the same effect:

The pillar of cloud also moved from in front and stood behind them, coming between the armies of Egypt and Israel. Throughout the night the cloud brought darkness to the one side and light to the other side; so neither went near the other all night long (Ex. 14:19-20, NIV).

Hugh Hefner's father was a minister. Joseph Stalin studied for the priesthood. Mao Tse-tung was taught by Christian missionaries. The light of Christ rejected becomes darkness.

Jesus' reply to the Pharisees is for all who disbelieve. He said that His claim is above natural laws of verification, because one cannot verify judicially the claim that He made. He said in effect, "You ask for two witnesses? My father and Myself."

(8:14-18). The Pharisees' immediate reaction was to ask, "Where is Your Father?" (v. 19) Jesus answered, "You know neither Me, nor My Father; if you knew Me, you would know My Father also" (v. 19).

If they wanted knowledge of God, it was necessary that they seek it through Christ. The same is true for us. As we look to Christ, the mysteries of deity begin to unfold for us.

Claiming the Light

To have the light of Christ is the ultimate necessity of life, yet many do not know how to get it or to keep it. How do we stay with the light? By following and by obeying. This is what Jesus was saying (v. 12), and what the cloud in the wilderness illustrated. When the Children of Israel looked to the cloud of fire in the wilderness, they were guided completely by the position of the light:

> Now on the day that the tabernacle was erected the cloud covered the tabernacle, the tent of the testimony, and in the evening it was like the appearance of fire over the tabernacle, until morning. So it was continuously; the cloud would cover it by day, and the appearance of fire by night.
>
> And whenever the cloud was lifted from over the tent, afterward the sons of Israel would then set out; and in the place where the cloud settled down, there the sons of Israel would camp. At the command of the Lord the sons of Israel would set out, and at the command of the Lord they would camp; as long as the cloud settled over the tabernacle, they remained camped. Even when the cloud lingered over the tabernacle for many days, the sons of Israel would keep the Lord's charge and not set out.
>
> If sometimes the cloud remained a few days over the tabernacle, according to the command of the Lord they remained camped. Then according to the command of the Lord they set out. If sometimes the cloud remained from evening until morning, when the cloud was lifted in the morning, they would move out; or if it remained in the daytime and at night, whenever the cloud was lifted, they would set out.

Whether it was two days or a month or a year that the cloud lingered over the tabernacle, staying above it, the sons of Israel remained camped and did not set out; but when it was lifted, they did set out (Num. 9:15-22).

The only way to possess the light of Christ is to learn submission to Him. This is not something we learn once and then claim to have mastered. In my own experience I have found there are times when the joy and the power leave my life and I feel confusion or weariness. It is in those times that I find relief only in submission to God, that I take everything and lay it before God and say, "I give up. It is Your ministry. It is Your Word. My work in the ministry is Yours—not mine." Then I find rest and peace, power and joy.

It may be that you have never laid your burden, your work, before the Lord. If that is true, I encourage you to do so. Then stay under the cloud of fire. Don't run ahead of it or lag behind. This kind of living requires faith and submission to the will of God—not once, but day by day.

If you have never experienced the light of life, you too need to take a step of submission and obedience, as you submit yourself to the truth. John said of Jesus, "As many as received Him, to them He gave the right to become children of God, even to those who believe in His name" (John 1:12).

In submission, realize that you are a sinner, repent of your sin, submit yourself to the cleansing blood of Christ, admitting that within you there is nothing that commends you to God. In this submission you will begin to walk in the light as the life of Christ becomes yours.

21
Ultimate Ancestry

In September of 1873, an unusual gathering took place in the resort town of Stockbridge, Massachusetts. Close to 500 descendants of Jonathan Edwards arrived for a family reunion. They lunched under a great tent which was provided by Yale University, and then admired memorabilia from the Edwards family. They saw Sarah Edwards' wedding dress, the silver bowl from which Jonathan ate his nightly porridge, and they poked around the old house, which was substantially unchanged.

The family reunion boasted professors, business executives, government officials, ministers, and women of unusual beauty and force of personality. The mood of the reunion was expressed by the initiator of the gathering when he said, "Let God be praised for such a man." His remarks were followed by many laudatory speeches that stirred the pride of Jonathan Edwards' descendants. This was as prestigious a celebration of ancestry as has been held in North America. A study by the New York Genealogical and Historical Society concluded:

Probably no two people married since the beginning of the 18th century have been progenitors of so many distinguished persons as were Jonathan Edwards and Sarah Pierrepont (Elisabeth Dodds, *Marriage to a Difficult Man*, Westminster, p. 204).

One statistic about the family is rarely mentioned. In 1756, Jonathan and Sarah's daughter Esther gave birth to a boy. When her son was still a baby, Esther described him as "very sly and mischievous ... has more spriteliness than Sally ... handsomer, but not so good tempered ... very resolute and requires a good governor to bring him to terms" (Dodds, *Marriage to a Difficult Man*, p. 39).

These words were written about the infamous Aaron Burr, who as an adult took the life of Alexander Hamilton and then plotted to crown himself Emperor of Mexico. These wonderful genetic qualities and the godly heritage seemed to be demonically reversed in Aaron Burr. This is a compelling story, especially for Christians who have enjoyed generations of godly heritage. We may be descended from people who were shapers of current religious thought and defenders of the faith. We may be related to someone who is on the forefront of Christian work today.

The people to whom Jesus was talking had a proud heritage, and yet their spiritual health was not good. Godly ancestors do not insure faithful progeny. People with the most favorable spiritual background may be in spiritual bondage. When Jesus suggested this possibility to the people around Him, they refused even to consider it:

Jesus therefore was saying to those Jews who had believed Him, "If you abide in My Word, then you are truly disciples of Mine; and you shall know the truth, and the truth shall make you free" (John 8:31-32).

The Jews completely missed His point. Jesus was speaking on a spiritual level, but they were thinking physically. "They answered Him, 'We are Abraham's offspring, and have never yet been enslaved to anyone; how is it that You say, "You shall become free"?' " (v. 33)

The Jews were slaves, though they wouldn't admit it. They so hated what had happened to them over the centuries that they said in their soul of souls, "History may say it, others may say it, but we will not admit to being slaves!" It was a grievous insult to suggest to any Jew that he might be in slavery. In A.D. 73, when Jewish soldiers were defending the fortress of Masada, Eleazar gave forth this great cry: "Long ago [we] resolved never to be servants to the Romans, nor to any other than to God Himself." When all hope was lost, the defenders committed suicide (William Whiston, trans., *Josephus,* "The Wars of the Jews," Kregel Publications, p. 600).

Jesus was speaking to the people of His time about spiritual bondage, and they refused to hear. Today, 2,000 years later, most people are deaf to the suggestion that they are in bondage. The worse their condition, the more they resent being told. John Calvin said, "The greater the mass of vices anyone is buried under, the more fiercely and bombastically does he extol free will."

We see this tendency in an alcoholic. "Me, an alcoholic? I can stop anytime. Where did you hide the bottle?"

If we suggest to a sensualist that he might be in bondage, he will probably retort that we are the ones in bondage—to archaic conventions and a repressive lifestyle.

People don't want to believe they are slaves, so they become desensitized to their true conditions. They minimize their enslavement with, "We've got to make a few adjustments."

In the secular media, we hear societal sin described as "cultural neurosis." But nowhere does the definition of sin sound more bizarre than in the world of theology, when the clergy do away with the profoundness of man's bondage. Lacking both sin and forgiveness, they end up in a theological wonderland (fantasyland).

Jesus held out the possibility of freedom to the Jewish people, but they ignored the spiritual meaning of His words and retorted that Abraham was their father.

Jesus' answer is as blunt a statement as appears in the Gospels. He clearly separated their physical ancestry from their spiritual heritage, and in essence told them that while they were physically children of Abraham, they were spiritually children of the devil:

> I know that you are Abraham's offspring; yet you seek to kill Me, because My word has no place in you. I speak the things which I have seen with My Father; therefore you also do the things which you heard from your father (vv. 37-38).

Physical Claims to Legitimacy

They again resorted to Abraham by saying, "Abraham is our father" (v. 39). The common belief at the time was that Abraham was so godly that he had stored up a vast treasury of merit from which his descendants could draw to attain righteousness.

Some years later, Trypho the Jew alluded to this belief in conversation with Justin Martyr. He claimed that the eternal kingdom would be given to those who are the seed of Abraham according to the flesh, even though they be sinners and unbelievers and disobedient to God. Abraham was spiritual security.

> Jesus said to them, "If you are Abraham's children, do the deeds of Abraham. But as it is, you are seeking to kill Me, a man who has told you the truth, which I heard from God; this Abraham did not do" (vv. 39-40).

The distinguishing mark of Abraham was that he responded to God when he heard the truth and was obedient. The Jews who confronted Jesus were living proof that they were not spiritual descendants of Abraham, by attempting to kill the bearer of truth.

When we apply these words to ourselves, we are reminded that the faith of our parents will not insure eternal life for us. The only substantive measure of our faith is what we do. This matter we must answer individually.

A godly heritage is of inestimable worth. I am a devoted student of preachers and preaching, and I have discovered that great preachers are often third and fourth generation ministers. Charles Spurgeon was the fourth generation, as was G. Campbell Morgan. If we have learned from our parents how to pray, how blessed we are. If we receive a missionary burden from our grandparents, we are again blessed. The privilege of such heritage is so great that it seems almost unfair to those Christians who do not have it. Yet if the heritage is not appropriated and lived out on a practical level, it can become a curse.

> His daughter's idol, and his wife's—
> the pictures blend and blur.
> At eighty, unregenerate,
> he died, in character:
> "God's pardon?" "On that subject I
> am coy," said Aaron Burr.
> (Dodd, *Marriage to a Difficult Man*, p. 183)

Claim to Legitimacy

When Jesus said that they were doing the deeds of their father, they understood what He meant, and retorted, "We were not born of fornication; we have one Father, even God" (v. 41).

Tragically, they supposed that God was their spiritual Father, when, indeed, He was not.

When the blessing of the heritage is not personalized, it can become a curse. We see this in instances where a parent is so desirous that a child become a Christian that the child professes Christ to please the parent rather than because of any reality of faith. Or the parents may so desire spiritual life for their children that they imagine the children possessing virtues they do not have.

The famous Cambridge professor Edmund Gosse tells how he finally rejected the godly heritage and faith of his parents. In one particularly sad chapter he recounts how his loving father was so desirous that his ten-year-old be baptized that he convinced the elders to interview Edmund.

I sat on a sofa in full lamplight and testified my faith in the Atonement with a fluency that surprised myself (so that my interviewer) . . . was weeping like a child (Edmund Gosse, *Father and Son*, W.W. Norton & Co., p. 145).

It was a perfect performance, but Edmund Gosse did not have grace in his life.

Some people in believing that their baptism placed them into a covenant relationship with God, have appropriated a false security and are in the same situation as the people of Jesus' day.

In Jesus' answer, we see three characteristics of the person who is not spiritually related to Christ.

• Lack of love for Christ,
• Unresponsiveness to the Word of God,
• Disobedience to God.

If God were your Father, you would love Me; for I proceeded forth and have come from God, for I have not even come on My own initiative, but He sent Me (v. 42).

In saying, "You would love Me," Christ was asserting that they did not. The highest test of faith is if we love Jesus Christ as He is presented to us in the Scriptures. Does your love for Christ transcend your love for all other people, ambitions, and objects? If not, you may not be related spiritually to God.

Why do you not understand what I am saying? It is because you cannot hear My word (v. 43).

He who is of God hears the words of God; for this reason you do not hear them, because you are not of God (v. 47).

Deafness and Disobedience

The second characteristic is spiritual deafness. Such people can analyze the sentences but they do not hear with their inner selves. The Word of God has no effect in their lives.

You are of your father the devil, and you want to do the desires of your father. He was a murderer from the beginning, and does not stand in the truth, because there is no truth in him. Whenev er he speaks a lie, he speaks from his own nature; for he is a liar, and the father of lies (v. 44).

The third characteristic is disobedience. Children of Satan are not desirous of doing God's will. This is not to suggest that Satan's children all consciously wish to serve him. Very few ever come to that. Rather, they serve themselves. They usually do not fall to Satan's levels of malevolence, but neither do they have any interest in the will of God.

Becoming God's Children

Satan is above all a deceiver, and those who follow him are characterized by deceit. They deceive themselves about their own hearts and about life. They deceive themselves about God and about the way of salvation, and some of them imagine that they are children of God when indeed they are not. This is the ultimate deception.

What are we personally to make of such strong teaching? Simply this: we are of one Father or the other. Regardless of our heritage, regardless of what other people tell us, we are either children of Satan or children of God. While I cannot imagine a wise person who would attempt to apply these tests to another, I cannot imagine a wise person who would not hold himself up to them, asking,

- Do I truly love Jesus?
- Does His Word have a place in me?
- Has He changed my life substantively?

If so, praise Him for the validation of your faith; if not, acknowledge your lack of love, your insensitivity to His Word, your unchanged life, and ask Him to meet you in your sin and remove it as far as the east is from the west. Trust Him alone for your salvation. Receive the ultimate ancestry.

But as many as received Him, to them He gave the right to become children of God, even to those who believe in His name; who were born not of blood, nor of the will of the flesh, nor of the will of man, but of God (John 1:12-13).

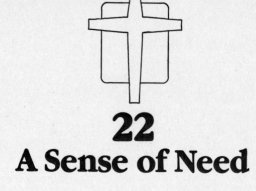

22
A Sense of Need

After Jesus had proclaimed Himself the Water of Life and the Light of the World, He left the temple and saw a man who had been blind from birth. Jesus must have fixed His gaze on the man, because the attention of the disciples was drawn to him so that they asked, "Rabbi, who sinned, this man or his parents, that he should be born blind?" (John 9:2)

It was a common Jewish belief that such physical defects had immediate hereditary causes. Some people even traced deformities to sin in the womb! Jesus answered: "It was neither that this man sinned nor his parents; but it was in order that the works of God might be displayed in him" (v. 3). He would not be involved in such profitless discussion.

"We must work the works of Him who sent Me, as long as it is day; night is coming, when no man can work. While I am in the world, I am the Light of the world" (vv. 4-5).

Jesus set the stage for what He was about to do.

Christ's Light at Work

This man who had never known light reminds us of Helen Keller who said, "Gradually I got used to the silence and darkness that surrounded me and forgot that it had ever been different, until she came—my teacher—who set my spirit free" (Helen Keller, *The Story of My Life*, Riverside Press, p. 8).

Perhaps people had told the blind man that light is bright, but he had no real idea what they were talking about. He could not conceive of blue or red. A million glories of nature were hidden from him—the green of spring grass, the magic of a sunset. As a child, he must have reached up and felt the softness of his mother's face, and maybe even a tear on her cheek, but he did not know what she looked like.

On this day, as Jesus had walked out of the temple, the blind beggar had heard, "While I am in the world, I am the Light of the world" (v. 5). In the silence that followed, the blind man heard someone kneel close to him and softly spit on the ground. Then he felt gentle hands applying the moist clay to his eyes and heard that same voice say, "Go, wash in the pool of Siloam" (v. 7).

I wonder if the blind man felt somewhat foolish. Even though he was sightless, he must have had some idea that he was creating a scene as he navigated toward the pool, his eyes covered with mud. I think his heart began to pound with the swelling possibility that he just might receive his sight. "What if it really works?" As he washed his eyes in the Pool of Siloam, light poured into his being with intensity. He could see!

I doubt that he had any thoughts of returning to begging. As he started back toward the temple, he gained speed and confidence. How happy everyone would be! But it wasn't quite that way:

The neighbors therefore, and those who previously saw him as a beggar, were saying, "Is not this the one who used to sit and beg?" Others were saying, "This is he," still others were saying,

"No, but he is like him." He kept saying, "I am the one" (vv. 8-9).

When he convinced the people that he was truly the formerly blind man, their discussion turned to how the miracle had occurred:

"How then were your eyes opened?" He answered, "The man who is called Jesus made clay, and annointed my eyes, and said to me, 'Go to Siloam, and wash'; so I went away and washed, and I received sight" (vv. 10-11).

None of them had ever heard of a person born blind receiving his sight. Even today that is true. I asked opthalmologists in my congregation about this and they all said that they had no knowledge of a congenitally blind person receiving sight, except for those few born with cataracts, in which case the sight is never fully restored.

Jesus performed a complete restoration of sight for this man. In the Gospel of John, the miracles of Jesus are always signs that teach deeper spiritual truths. This miracle teaches us about spiritual sight—how to receive it and maintain it. On the one side is a physically blind man who receives physical sight and then spiritual sight. On the other side are men who can see but who are spiritually blind. In these two extremes, we see the light of Christ received and rejected.

Christ's Light Rejected

Following the miracle were three ludicrous interrogations—two of the blind man and one of his parents. The first questions centered on the fact that Jesus had mixed the clay on the Sabbath—a specific sin according to rabbinic law. This was an attempt to dismiss Jesus as a sinner, till someone reminded the Pharisees that sinners cannot heal blind eyes (vv. 13-16).

The second interrogation was of the man's parents, in the

hope of uncovering a discrepancy in the story. However, the parents were so terrified that all they would say was, "He is of age; ask him" (vv. 18-23).

Finally, the Pharisees called back the man who had received his sight, and ordered him, "Give glory to God; we know that this man is a sinner" (v. 24). At this point, the man turned the tables on his questioners with a most adept response.

So for the second time they called in the man who had been blind and told him, "Give the glory to God, not to Jesus, for we know Jesus is an evil person."

"I don't know whether He is good or bad," the man replied, "but I know this: I was blind, and now I see!"

"But what did He do?" they asked. "How did He heal you?"

"Look!" the man exclaimed. "I told you once; didn't you listen? Why do you want to hear it again? Do you want to become His disciples too?"

Then they cursed him and said, "You are His disciple, but we are disciples of Moses. We know God has spoken to Moses, but as for this fellow, we don't know anything about Him."

"Why, that's very strange!" the man replied. "He can heal blind men, and yet you don't know anything about him! Well, God doesn't listen to evil men, but He has open ears to those who worship Him and do His will. Since the world began there has never been anyone who could open the eyes of someone born blind. If this Man were not from God, He couldn't do it."

"You illegitimate bastard, you!" they shouted. "Are you trying to teach *us?*" And they threw him out.

When Jesus heard what had happened, he found the man and said, "Do you believe in the Messiah?"

The man answered, "Who is He, Sir, for I want to "

"You have seen Him," Jesus said, "and He is speaking to you!"

"Yes, Lord," the man said, "I believe!" And he worshiped Jesus (vv. 23-38, TLB).

With oaths and aspersions on the legitimacy of his birth, they had ousted him. The Pharisees rejected the witness of the

Light. Commenting on this St. John Chrysostom wrote: "The Jews cast him out of the temple, and the Lord of the temple found him."

Christ's Light Received

Jesus came to the man and worked the second great miracle for him—his conversion. Then the man possessed spiritual light as well. He saw with his heart, as well as with his eyes.

Those who claimed to have spiritual sight were still blind. The question comes today—as it did then—why is it that people who really care about spiritual matters at times remain blind to the truth? The Pharisees cared so much that they had subjected every area of their lives to their religious beliefs. Jesus answered this for the people of His day and for us. "For judgment I came into this world, that those who do not see may see; and that those who see may become blind" (v. 39).

Christ came to earth so that those who think they have spiritual insight may be shown to be blind, and those who do not suppose they have this spiritual insight may see. His whole argument centered around a person's sense of need. If someone felt no need, he would not see; but those who knew they were blind were the ones who could be made to see.

The Pharisees who heard Him asked, "We are not blind too, are we?" (v. 40) Jesus answered, "If you were blind, you would have no sin; but now you say, 'We see,' your sin remains" (v. 41). In other words, "Because you have some spiritual ligh you are blamable. And because you are self-satisfied and say 'We see,' you are unhealable." This truth gives rise to the spiritual axioms: Those who go blind are the ones who do not realize their need. Those who receive sight are the ones who sense their darkness.

Through their acquaintance with the Law, the Pharisees believed they were sinners, but they did not understand how deeply infected with sin they were. They adopted the external appearance of having dealt with the sin when, indeed, they had never faced the darkness of their hearts. In their self-satisfaction, they said, "We see," when they were really blind.

In his introduction to *Screwtape Letters,* C.S. Lewis wrote:

> Some have paid me an undeserved compliment by supposing that my *Letters* were the ripe fruit of many years' study in moral and ascetic theology. They forgot that there is an equally reliable, though less creditable, way of learning how temptation works. "My heart"—I need no other's—"showeth me the wickedness of the ungodly" (C.S. Lewis, *The Screwtape Letters and Screwtape Proposes a Toast,* Macmillan, p. 13).

That this was not the style of the Pharisees, we see in Jesus' parable about the two men who went up to the temple to pray. One was a Pharisee and one a tax-gatherer. The Pharisee prayed, "God, I thank Thee that I am not like other people: swindlers, unjust, adulterers, or even like this tax-gatherer. I fast twice a week; I pay tithes of all that I get" (Luke 18:11-12).

But the tax-gatherer, unwilling to lift his eyes to heaven, prayed, "God, be merciful to me, the sinner!" (v. 13) Not *a* sinner, but *the* sinner. Religious know-it-alls who believe they see, remain blind. No hope exists for the soul that desires to stay in ignorance of its sin, preferring his own darkened understanding.

On Receiving Christ's Light

The blind man knew his need. "I see" was not part of his vocabulary. And because it was not, he knew he was in the dark. He knew that the darkness was spiritual as well as physical. He sensed his own insufficiency and had the humility to admit his need.

It is conceivable that he could have felt great pride in his disadvantaged status, or in his prowess as a beggar, and have been the equivalent morally of the person who prides himself in his insight or ethical judgments and yet remains blind to God.

The basis of spiritual growth is an awareness of the natural darkness of our hearts—the need for the light of Christ. Jesus began the Sermon on the Mount, "Blessed are the poor in spirit, for theirs is the kingdom of heaven" (Matt. 5:3). Blessed are those who realize that they have nothing within themselves that commends them to God.

Alexander Whyte was a great Scottish preacher of the 19th century. One day a man came to tell him about an evangelist who was preaching in Edinburgh and criticizing local ministers. The man told Dr. Whyte that the evangelist had said that Dr. Hood Wilson was not a Christian. When Whyte heard that, he leaped out of his chair and exclaimed, "The rascal! Dr. Wilson not a converted man?" Then the man continued, "And that is not all. He said that you are not converted either." At that, Whyte stopped short, sat back down in his chair, and put his face in his hands. After a long silence, he said, "Leave me, friend, leave me! I must examine my heart!" (Warren Wiersbe, *Walking with the Giants,* Baker, p. 92)

The kingdom of God belongs to those who realize that within themselves is nothing to commend them to God. They are happy because their emptiness is the occasion for God's fullness.

It is not our littleness that hinders Christ; but our bigness. It is not our weakness that hinders Christ; it is our strength. It is not our darkness that hinders Christ; it is our supposed light that holds back His hand (Charles Spurgeon, *Metropolitan Tabernacle Pulpit,* Vol. 30, p. 489).

The way of the blind beggar is the way to sight. He did not argue with Christ. He owned his condition of blindness. He submitted himself to the hands of Christ, was obedient to His Word, and received the miracle of sight to his eyes and to his heart.

Let Christ lighten your darkness and fill your emptiness, so that the works of God may be displayed in you.

23
The Beautiful Shepherd

In his book, *A Shepherd Looks at Psalm 23,* Philip Keller explains how utterly helpless sheep are. They are of limited intelligence, are uncreative about finding food, and are such creatures of habit that they will follow paths through the most desolate places, even though excellent forage is not far away. Sheep are given to endless wandering and some have even walked into fires.

In temperament, sheep are more timid than stubborn and can be frightened by ridiculous things. Because they have no means of self-defense, caring for them is an enormous amount of work. Keller describes a danger unique to sheep—being cast down or simply, cast. A cast sheep cannot get back on its feet.

Even the largest, fattest, strongest, and sometimes healthiest sheep can become cast and be a casualty. The way it happens is this. A heavy, fat, or long-fleeced sheep will lie down comfortably in some little hollow or depression in the ground. It may roll on its side slightly to stretch out or relax. Suddenly the center of gravity in the body shifts so that it turns on its back far enough that the feet no longer touch the ground. It may feel a sense of panic and start to paw frantically. Frequently this only makes things worse. It rolls over even further. Now it is quite impossible for it to regain its feet (Zondervan, p. 61).

Some years ago, two couples from our church, Clem and Laura Jervis and Clarence and Betty Wyngarden, were vacationing in England. One afternoon they drove back deep into the Cotswolds. As they were delighting in the scenery, Dr. Wyngarden noticed a flock of sheep. One of the sheep was away from the rest, with all of its feet up in the air. Clarence thought, "It must be dead." But as they drove on, he remembered what he had heard about a sheep being cast, and thought, "I bet that is a cast sheep." He told Clem what he thought and Clem said that Clarence read too much. They discussed the matter and finally turned around to investigate. As they got out of the car and walked toward the animal, they found a fat and pregnant sheep, unshorn, overloaded with wool, lying on her back, bleating for help.

Clarence did what every good doctor does: he took a picture (which now hangs in my study). Then he decided he would take yet another picture while Clem turned the sheep over onto her feet, but Clem could not manage alone. It took both of them to set that poor ewe back on her feet, and when they finally did get her up, she staggered around for some time trying to get her balance. They steadied her and, good doctor that he is, Clarence massaged her legs to get her circulation going again. At last, she bleated her thank-you and wandered off toward the flock. Clem and Clarence said they learned something from this: sheep are not possibly helpless or theoretically helpless—they are absolutely helpless.

When Jesus chose an animal to characterize human nature, He picked sheep: helpless, wandering, and often cast down. In this context Jesus said of Himself, "I am the Good Shepherd" (John 10:11). The people who heard Jesus knew shepherding to be an intimate, highly personal occupation. The Palestinian shepherd did not drive his sheep; rather he went before them and led them. A shepherd would typically tend his sheep for years, calling each of his flock by name. The very survival of the sheep depended on the shepherd's hour-by-hour care.

To the ancient mind, there was no greater picture of lostness than of sheep without a shepherd. Jesus used this figure to describe the crowds who followed Him: "And seeing the multitudes, He felt compassion for them, because they were distressed and downcast like sheep without a shepherd" (Matt. 9:36).

The Shepherd Relates to His Sheep

> Truly, truly, I say to you, he who does not enter by the door into the fold of the sheep, but climbs up some other way, he is a thief and a robber. But he who enters by the door is a shepherd of the sheep. To him the doorkeeper opens; and the sheep hear his voice; and he calls his own sheep by name, and leads them out (John 10:1-3).

Jewish shepherds kept their sheep in two kinds of sheepfolds. Out in the country the folds were low-walled corrals made of stone with a narrow opening in front. In the city, sheepfolds were much larger, more soundly constructed, and were often communal corrals. These had professional gatekeepers who knew all the shepherds who kept their sheep there.

It is this communal corral to which Jesus referred in John 10. The shepherd arrives at the gate and is recognized by the gatekeeper and admitted into the fold. As he walks among the mixed flock, the uninitiated would wonder how he would ever find his own sheep. But as he begins to talk, in the characteristic sing-song that only his sheep would respond to, they come near to him and follow him out to the pasture.

The voice of the shepherd is vitally important to the sheep. Even when shepherds exchanged clothes to see if they could trick the sheep, when they spoke, the sheep knew who they were.

Jesus also spoke of the shepherd calling each sheep by name. Palestinian shepherds called their sheep by their characteristics. One might be Long Nose and another Black Ear or another Fluffy. This is an appealing picture, for it shows us how our Lord is aware of our individual characteristics and knows us each by name.

This is just a hint of the familiarity that the sheep have with the shepherd. Jesus said, "I am the Good Shepherd; and I know My own, and My own know Me, even as the Father knows Me and I know the Father" (vv. 14-15). Jesus knows us as He knows His Father, with intimate knowledge. No relationship is more intimate than that between God the Father and God the Son, and it is with this indivisible union and eternal intimacy that Jesus knows His own. That very quality of Jesus' knowledge of the Father is extended to us, reaching into the deepest parts of our lives, going back before birth. Of this divine knowledge, the psalmist wrote.

> My frame was not hidden from Thee, when I was made in secret, and skillfully wrought in the depths of the earth. Thine eyes have seen my unformed substance; and in Thy Book they were all written, the days that were ordained for me, when as yet there was not one of them (139:15-16).

Jesus knows us in the profoundest ways. He knows our past failures and hurts, He knows our present unrealized longings. He knows our idiosyncrasies and calls us by our characteristics, maybe even by those names that show our weaknesses.

Knowing the Shepherd

Yet the wonder is not only that Jesus knows us, but that we can know Him. As His sheep, we hear His voice and respond to Him in a relationship that holds the same possibility of familiarity that exists between the Father and the Son. Most of us know Him better than we think we do. We hear His voice and we know His will and are aware of His constant provision for us.

A story is told about the great Swedish filmmaker, Ingmar Bergman. One day as he was listening to Stravinsky, he had a vision of a nineteenth-century cathedral. Bergman saw himself wandering about in the cathedral and finally coming to a picture of Christ. Realizing the importance of seeing Christ, Bergman said to the picture, "Speak to me! I will not leave this cathedral until You speak to me!" Of course, the picture did not respond and this deeply affected Bergman. Within that same year, he produced *The Silence,* a film about people who despair of ever finding God.

Our Good Shepherd says of Himself: "When He puts forth all His own, He goes before them, and the sheep follow Him because they know His voice" (John 10:4). To Ingmar Bergman, to us, He offers the deepest, most satisfying of relationships, one that cannot exist between mortals, and one which is the foundational reality of our existence.

The Shepherd Provides

Jesus therefore said to them again, "Truly, truly, I say to you, I am the door of the sheep. All who come before Me are thieves and robbers, but the sheep did not hear them. I am the door; if anyone enters through Me, he shall be saved, and shall go in and out, and find pasture. The thief comes only to steal, and kill, and destroy; I came that they might have life, and might have it abundantly" (vv. 7-10).

While G. Campbell Morgan was traveling across the Atlantic by steamer, he visited with Sir George Adam Smith, a famous Old Testament scholar. Sir George told of a conversation with a shepherd who showed him the fold into which the sheep were led at night It consisted of four walls, with a way in.

Sir George said to him, "That is where they go at night?" "Yes," said the shepherd, "and when they are in there, they are perfectly safe." "But there is no door," said Sir George. "I am the door," said the shepherd. He was not a Christian man; he was not speaking in the language of the New Testament. He was speaking from the Arab shepherd's standpoint. Sir George looked at him and said, "What do you mean by the door?" Said the shepherd, "When the light is gone, and all the sheep are inside, I lie in the open space, and no sheep ever goes out but across my body, and no wolf comes in unless he crosses my body; I am the door" (G. Campbell Morgan, *The Gospel According to John*, Fleming H. Revell, p. 177).

This is the meaning of Jesus' words, "I am the door." He was actually saying, "I am the living door. In order to go into the fold, you must go through Me. To go out to pasture, you must go through Me. As the door, I am the protector and I am the provider. When you come in the door, you are not only saved, but you are safe. When you go out through Me, you go out to pasture. I am the provider. Nobody is coming through that door except he comes through Me."

In speaking of finding pasture and of abundant life, Jesus is not promising an abundance of things (vv. 9-10). Rather, the image is one of the Great Shepherd leading His sheep into the green pastures beside the still waters, of His pursuing the stray sheep, keeping them away from harm, leading them to good water, making sure they find life and abundance and health. Is this only for brilliant sheep? Beautiful sheep? Energetic sheep? No. It is a promise for all those who follow where their Shepherd leads, believing that He knows what is best for them.

The Shepherd Loves

I am the Good Shepherd; the Good Shepherd lays down His life for the sheep. He who is a hireling, and not a shepherd, who is not the owner of the sheep, beholds the wolf coming, and leaves the sheep, and flees, and the wolf snatches them, and scatters them. He flees because he is a hireling, and is not concerned about the sheep.

I am the Good Shepherd; and I know My own, and My own know Me, even as the Father knows Me and I know the Father; and I lay down My life for the sheep. And I have other sheep, which are not of this fold; I must bring them also, and they shall hear My voice; and they shall become one flock with one Shepherd.

For this reason the Father loves Me, because I lay down My life that I may take it again. No one has taken it away from Me, but I lay it down on My own initiative. I have authority to lay it down, and I have authority to take it up again. This commandment I received from My Father (vv. 11-18).

We read four times that Christ lays down His life for the sheep. Such is a shepherd's heart. Christ was always laying down His life. He devoted His life to His people and finally of His own initiative gave His life in an act of supreme sacrifice. In Gethsemane, the soldiers did not capture Him. His very words cast them back, yet He gave Himself up to them. The Scripture describes His death on the cross, He "yielded up His spirit" (Matt. 27:50). Our Lord glories in His substitutionary death for us. And we can say, with the Apostle Paul, "May it never be that I should boast, except in the cross of our Lord Jesus Christ, through which the world has been crucified to me and I to the world" (Gal. 6:14).

In the Greek words of John 10:11, 14, which are translated "I am the Good Shepherd," there is rich meaning because the word for Good is the *kalos* which better translates "beautiful," so that some translators render the phrase "I am the Shepherd, the beautiful Shepherd." The Shepherd is both good and beautiful—and much more. Spurgeon caught the feeling of this when he wrote:

There is more in Jesus, the Good Shepherd, than you can pack away in a shepherd. He is the good, the great, the chief Shepherd; but He's much more. Emblems to set Him forth may be multiplied as the drops of the morning, but the whole multitude will fail to reflect all His brightness. Creation is too small a frame in which to hang His likeness. Human thought is too contracted, human speech too feeble, to set Him forth to the full. When all the emblems in earth and heaven shall have described Him to their utmost, there will remain a somewhat not yet described. You may square the circle ere you can set forth Christ in the language of mortal men. He is inconceivably above our conceptions, unutterably above our utterances (*The Metropolitan Tabernacle Pulpit,* C.H. Spurgeon, Vol. 32, Pilgrim, p. 3).

Such is the Shepherd we proclaim. He is altogether beautiful because of the way He relates to us and knows us; because we know Him and because He sees to our needs. He is beautiful because He is the door through whom we pass to find protection and salvation, green pastures, and abundant life. He is beautiful because of His heart of love that caused Him to lay down His life for His sheep. His heart is so expansive that He offers us all a place in His fold.

And I have other sheep, which are not of this fold; I must bring them also, and they shall hear My voice; and they shall become one flock with one Shepherd (John 10:16).

Your name is in the Bible, right in this verse. And so is mine. I am one of the "other sheep." Yet even better, before the foundation of the world, my name was written in God's Book, and so was yours, if you respond to Him as your Shepherd.

If you want to be one of those who lives in the relationship, provision, and love of the Shepherd, submit yourself to Him as Lord and Bishop of your soul. To pass through the door of Christ's death for you is the hardest thing in all the world because it means renouncing yourself and your work. It means following Him who is the way, the truth, the life, the door, the beautiful Shepherd, and the one who alone is the door to abundant life.